About the authors

After moving to Italy and Hong Kong with _____ years-old, Lisa Clifford returned to Australia in her early 20s to win the radio scholarship award in journalism at the Australian Film, TV and Radio School. The ABC's Radio National needed an Italian correspondent to work on The Europeans programme, Lisa got the job and returned to Italy for another two years. But she describes herself as an Aussie outdoors girl at heart so the thought of clean air and white beaches ultimately lured her back to settle in Australia. Five years as a reporter and editor for 2UW and 2GB followed. Several years of on-air TV news reporting for Channel 10 was then the natural progression and Lisa is now the Associate Producer of Channel 10's Late News. She is also a fanatical walker.

Journalist/Television producer of some 30 years, Mandy Webb was born in New Zealand and came to Australia to pursue her career aged 20. Based in Sydney, Mandy has produced news, current affairs and lifestyle programmes for ABC Television and Channel 10. She was Chief of Staff at Channel 10 during the state's worst bushfires; went on tour with Prince Charles and has produced a Sydney to Hobart yacht race. Finding herself between jobs last year, Mandy took the opportunity to follow a lifetime passion — walking in the great Aussie outdoors and writing about it.

Lisa Clifford and Mandy Webb would like
to thank everyone that made *Walking Sydney*
possible. For the photography we are
extremely grateful to Dave Arthur, Bill
Counsell, Daniele Mattioli, Tim Clifford and
Martin Webby. For all their help with the
book we thank Pip Grant Taylor, Janet
DeBris, Jervis Sparks of Barrenjoey
Lighthouse, Cath Hamey of The Balmain
Association, Maureen Smith of Manly
Library, the Rocks Authority and the
Darling Harbour Authority; as well as the
local history sections of Willoughby,
Maroobra, Pittwater and Waverley
Libraries. Thanks also to the National Parks
and Wildlife Service and to all the road-
testers who gave so freely of their time.

First published 1997 in Pan by Pan
Macmillan Australia Pty Limited
St Martins Tower, 31 Market Street, Sydney

Reprinted 1997

National Library of Australia
Cataloguing-in-Publication data:

Clifford, Lisa
Walking Sydney

ISBN 0 330 36022 1

1. Walking – New South Wales – Sydney –
Guidebooks. 2. Sydney (NSW) –
Guidebooks. I. Webb, Mandy. II. Title.

919. 4410465

Designed by Big Cat Design
Printed in Australia by McPherson's
Printing Group

Walking Sydney

LISA CLIFFORD AND MANDY WEBB

PAN
Pan Macmillan Australia

Map of the greater Sydney area showing the walks included in *Walking Sydney*

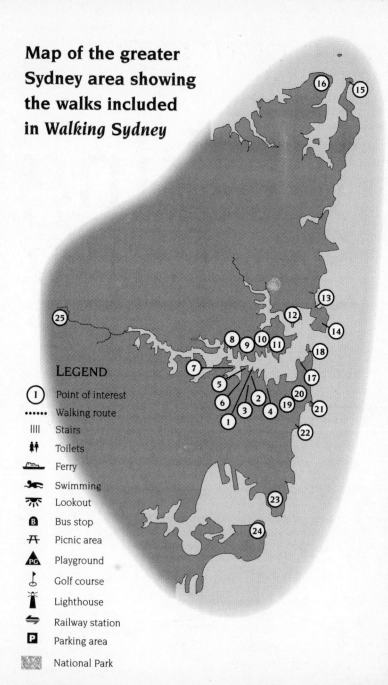

LEGEND

①	Point of interest
••••••	Walking route
‖‖‖	Stairs
👥	Toilets
🚢	Ferry
🏊	Swimming
🔭	Lookout
Ⓑ	Bus stop
⊼	Picnic area
PG	Playground
⛳	Golf course
🗼	Lighthouse
🚆	Railway station
P	Parking area
▦	National Park

CONTENTS

INTRODUCTION

*t*his book leads you to Sydney's most beautiful areas. It's a collection of 25 walks that take you on an adventure of discovery — to beaches, cliffs, bushland and colonial cobblestoned streets. Some routes cover the heart of the city's centre, others lead you to romantic shoreline tracks. Each one brings you closer to knowing Sydney's soul. The walks are designed to give you an insight into Australia's unique culture through a fascinating and detailed commentary about the places of interest along the way. This book involves the reader in a journey of virtual reality, you'll pass through time to the different eras and special moments of Sydney's past to experience the history for yourself.

Many of the following stories are about Sydney's Aborigines — the masters of Walkabout. Within three years of colonisation, their numbers were decimated. But Sydney's Aborigines left behind many clues to their culture. Bondi in Darug dialect means the sound of tumbling water, whereas Manly was named by the first white people because the natives there appeared so masculine. Where possible, we track their traditional land and tell you of their customs.

Walking Sydney's routes are simple and accessible. Check the map of Sydney opposite the contents page and choose the area you'd most like to explore. Read the walk's summary to find out more about your destination then refer to its key, to make sure you have enough time and energy to embark on it.

This book is not just aimed at giving readers a fun day outdoors, it's also about the world's most underrated sport — walking. Doing it for just half an hour each day will have a dramatic effect on your life. Control your weight, stress and posture by striding out everyday. The risk of osteoporosis and heart disease falls every time you do. A daily walking routine tones up those saggy muscles, improves your skin tone, makes you look and feel terrific — and improves your confidence! Devise your own daily walking plan and let *Walking Sydney* spur you along by weaving a yarn into your special expeditions.

PLANNING TO WALK SYDNEY

Beware! The Aussie outdoors is hard, hot and dry in summer — so hats and sunscreen are essential. Australia's unique environment means walkers need to think ahead. If you burn easily, wear a light, long sleeved cotton shirt and trousers. This is also a good idea if you're heading to parklands where the bush is prickly. In winter the outdoors looks inviting, but can be deceptively cold, so take a woollen jumper and a light wind-proof parka. There are few cities in the world that offer views and beaches as spectacular as Sydney. Consider taking:

- *a light frameless backpack with*
- *SPF15+ sunscreen and a hat that protects your neck and shoulders*
- *sunglasses*
- *fly repellent*
- *water,*
- *swimmers and towel*
- *a camera*
- *a pocket knife*
- *a picnic, or light snack*

Wearing the right gear is most important, beginning and ending with your feet. A good walk is a comfortable walk and ill-fitting, inappropriate footwear can do a walker serious damage. Good fitting running shoes are okay, but a specially designed walking shoe is better. The actions of running and walking are completely different. Runners land with 3 to 4 times their body weight every time their feet hit the ground. By contrast, walkers land with only 1 to 1.5 times their weight. Here's a checklist for the right walking shoe:

- *uppers of high quality material that breathes — such as leather or nylon mesh*
- *a comfortable padded heel collar*
- *a firm heel counter that cups the heel to give stability for the entire foot and leg*
- *a sole to absorb shock*
- *substantial arch supports*
- *a toe area that doesn't rub*

Walking Sydney is a Pan Macmillan book in association with Rockport Walking Shoes. Rockport designs an excellent range of shoes that are specifically designed to meet the demands of walkers. The project's aim is to discover Sydney by foot, then bring walkers home healthy, happy and keen to set out for their next walk.

HEALTH TIPS

Stretching is a really good idea before and after your walk — it's not just for super athletes. Do some simple stretches slowly for 5–7 minutes.

SPF15+ sunscreen should be applied before you start your walk — don't wait until you start burning before putting it on. Reapply sunscreen after a swim.

Drink fluids before leaving home and remember to sip from your water bottle often when out walking in the heat.

Your digestion system is an 'involuntary' one, so avoid walking after big meals as your body will dedicate its energy to digesting your food. The energised blood needed to power your muscles takes second place, until digestion is out of the way.

NATIONAL PARKS

Walking Sydney will take you through several National Parks. Please note the Park Rangers request that you:

- *stay on the walking tracks to minimise damage to wildflowers, vegetation and rocks*
- *leave the plants, animals shells and rocks where you found them and don't feed the wildlife*
- *leave historic places and Aboriginal sites undisturbed — don't walk on Aboriginal engravings or touch their paintings*
- *leave your pets at home*
- *take your rubbish home with you*
- *observe fire bans*
- *stay away from unfenced cliff edges and supervise your children*

NOTE: some of the National Park walks are isolated and we don't recommend you do them alone.

If walking causes you chest pain, see your doctor. Don't set out if you have flu or fever — your body needs rest not exercise.

Finally, take your time, enjoy the views and above all, have fun. Sydney is one of the most beautiful city's in the world — so lace up and let's go!

Walking
Sydney

WALK 1

THE OPERA HOUSE TO THE BOTANIC GARDENS

START POINT:	East Circular Quay.
FINISH:	The Opera House.
HOW TO GET THERE:	Circular Quay is a transit point for many bus, train and ferry services.
LENGTH:	Nearly 3 kilometres.
WALKING TIME:	2 hours.
ACTUAL TIME:	Including stops to take in the views and further explore the Botanic Gardens, this walk can take all day.
RATING:	Easy: a level, sealed path.
WEATHER CHECK:	There are lots of trees and leaves for protection if it rains, plus shelter under the Opera House and inside the Botanic Gardens restaurant and information centre.
REFRESHMENTS:	Restaurant and cafe within the Botanic Gardens.

Mostly suitable for wheelchairs and strollers.

the most famous of all walks in Australia, you're guaranteed a special excursion with this stroll around the Opera House, the Botanic Gardens and Mrs Macquarie's Chair. This walk looks at the growth of Farm Cove and its early European settlement, as well as the customs of the area's original residents. When Arthur Phillip arrived in Port Jackson in 1788, he found the harbour's Aboriginal people liked to live along its shoreline so they could fish and cook from their bark canoes and shelter under coastal caves. It was discovered that Farm Cove was where the Eora tribesmen held their manhood initiation ceremonies. Boys became men during the Kangaroo and Dog Dances along the shores of what is now the Botanic Gardens. Captain Phillip befriended a local Aboriginal man called Bennelong, who is one of Australia's most fondly remembered Aborigines. Bennelong's hut was on 'Limeburners Point', long before the Opera House. The walk takes you past the convict-built wall into the Botanic Gardens, one of Australia's top 20 attractions and known as Sydney's lungs. The gardens are a green city oasis with 7000 different types of plants. You'll cover some of the gardens' special sites, such as Sydney's first farm display, the I Wish statue and the glasshouses. After enjoying the view from Mrs Macquarie's favourite vantage point, we cut a path through the gardens to reach Government House, only recently opened to the public. The former residence of New South Wales governors, the house has become a symbol of the battle between monarchists and republicans.

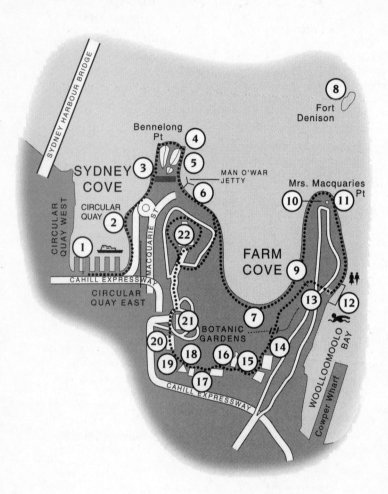

POINTS OF INTEREST ALONG THE WAY

(1) **Your start point is Circular Quay,** the place where Sydney was founded by the First Fleet in 1788. Originally, Sydney Cove's muddy beach stretched back about 100 metres towards the city. This area was first reclaimed in 1817 to give ships better berthing depth. Stone from the ridge in front of the Opera House was used to build the cove's walls.

(2) **Face Sydney Cove and turn east (right) and take the walkway along the water to the Opera House.** Along the eastern shoreline of the quay is one of the most severely criticised constructions of the 1990s. The 15-storey block of Colonial Mutual apartments crept up on Sydneysiders and protests went unheard — the money for the $200 million development had already been delivered and the contracts signed. Filling in the

> *The Sydney Harbour Bridge was completed in 1932. Excitement mounted during the ten years it took to build the single-span bridge, as it was going to be the world's longest. Just when it was about to be finished, however, New York completed their 'coat-hanger' which was 63 centimetres longer. Peak-hour traffic jams were commonplace until the underwater Harbour Tunnel was finished in the mid-1990s.*

precious space between the Opera House and the Botanic Gardens, the building has been labelled an unforgivable destruction of the area's ambience.

(3) **The Sydney Opera House** was designed by Danish architect Joern Utzon, who won an international competition launched in 1955. He said he got the idea from a pile of orange peel. The one million off-white tiles were imported from Sweden, the brown glass from France, and the rose-coloured granite on the podium was quarried at Tarana, near Bathurst, in New South Wales. The Opera Theatre is under the biggest sail and seats 1500. A series of lotteries paid for its construction.

(4) **First called Cattle Point because the First Fleet's animals were grazed here, Bennelong Point** was renamed after a lovable Aboriginal man called Bennelong. He lived in a hut here and was 'captured' or 'befriended' by Captain Arthur Phillip. In 1792 Phillip thought it was a great idea to take Bennelong and another Aboriginal man, Yemmerrawannie, back to England to meet King George III. The experience did not help to 'civilise' the men as Captain Phillip had hoped — Yemmerrawannie died after a year

in London and Bennelong came home a confused man. His age is unknown — it's thought he was 49 when he died in a tribal fight in 1813.

⑤ **Fort Macquarie occupied Bennelong Point** when there was a small rocky island off its tip. In 1817 convicts began building the fort with rocks from East Circular Quay. A dramatic drawbridge provided its only access to land. The purpose of the fort was to nab ships that hadn't paid port fees. After the fort's demolition in 1902, the point became a tram terminus and ultimately the land on which the Opera House was built.

⑥ **Continue around the Opera House forecourt through the elaborate wrought-iron Queen Elizabeth II gates to the Botanic Gardens, keeping to the shoreline path.** The stone seawall beside you is called the 30 Years Wall, because that's how long the convicts took to build it — from 1848 to 1879. The wall dammed mudflats that had

The Opera House ghost is seen regularly by staff who describe him as elderly and well presented in a greatcoat. He's often spotted in Box C, but only during the ballet season. Another famous theatregoer from the spiritual world is a poltergeist who regularly taps out a tempo to concerts. The tapping has been looked into, but no-one can find the source.

become putrid with sewage from Sydney's colonial residents. Originally Farm Cove beach started near the kiosk in the centre of the gardens.

The Aboriginal people held initiation ceremonies for their young males on the land near the tidal flats of Farm Cove. During the Kangaroo and Dog Dances an oval area was cleared so a tribal elder could dance with a grass-shaped kangaroo on his shoulders and lay it at the feet of the initiates. The young men stood in a circle while the men beat a rhythm on their shields and chanted. The boys had their right front tooth knocked out and a bone or reed inserted through their nose to symbolise their maturity.

⑦ **You are now in Farm Cove,** known to the Aboriginal people as Woccanmagully and to Sydneysiders as the Botanic Gardens. These 30 hectares were dedicated to growing Sydney's first crops. The concept for the gardens was crystallised in 1816 when Charles Fraser became Australia's first botanist. This is the Lower Garden, where a century ago a creek was dammed to create ponds and designer lawns.

⑧ **In front of you is Fort Denison,** which was a rocky island the natives called Mattewai, which means 'touch the sky'. The name was appropriate considering Mattewai Island was 25 metres high. Captain Phillip decided to send Sydney's

worst convicts there for solitary confinement. They were given only bread and water, so Mattewai became known as Pinchgut, though some say the name came from the nautical term for the narrowest point in a channel. In 1796, convict Francis Morgan was hanged from Mattewai's pinnacle — his skeleton swung in the wind for three years. The island became Fort Denison in 1857 after two American ships snuck into the harbour, which made the authorities realise how vulnerable the harbour was.

⑨ Pass the second set of gates and continue to Mrs Macquarie's Point. Beside the path are Moreton Bay fig trees, native to Australia's east coast. These ones were planted a century ago.

⑩ Mrs Macquarie's Chair is a little further around the point, an easily spotted seat carved into the sandstone cliff-face. The wife of Governor Lachlan Macquarie, Elizabeth loved to sit at this point and enjoy the views. Mrs Macquarie already had a well-developed passion for pathway planning after dabbling in it in her home town, Appin, in Scotland. She lived at Government House and had her husband order the road that leads here, and as a special treat she was given her own personal seat.

⑪ Follow the coastal path, which branches off below Mrs Mac's Chair (as it's affectionately known), around to Woolloomooloo Bay. Across the water is the Cowper Wharf and Garden Island Naval base, and beyond that is Kings Cross (see the Kings Cross Walk).

⑫ Follow the path where it branches up to the right at the Andrew 'Boy' Charlton Pool. Woolloomoolo Bay was a 19th and 20th century saltwater bathing resort, where the huge 1908 Domain Baths had a grandstand that seated 1600 people and 250 dressing sheds. The swimming tradition continues with the Andrew 'Boy' Charlton Pool. Here in 1924 Charlton set three world records in the 200, 400 and 800 metre freestyle races against world record holder Arne Borg. The Baths were renamed in his honour.

The Aboriginal people of Sydney Harbour ate enormous quantities of shellfish. In Sydney's early days Bennelong Point was also called Limeburners Point because it was covered in huge mounds of leftover mollusc shells from thousands of Aboriginal meals. These shells were gathered by convicts and burned in a kiln to provide the lime for the mortar to build Sydney's first buildings.

(13) **Walk over Mrs Macquarie's Road, where you'll see an entrance in the Botanic Gardens wall called the Victoria Lodge Gate entrance. Follow the signs to the Succulent Gardens.**

(14) **Pass through Macquarie's Wall.** Governor Macquarie was very territorial about his 'Domain'. By 1812 this wall stretched from Wolloomooloo Bay to Farm Cove and no-one was allowed inside it without his permission. Five years later two men were caught trespassing, and they were each given 25 lashes. The wall is now lined with swamp mahogany.

(15) **Next to the Succulent Gardens is the Botanic Gardens information centre. From here follow the signs to the Tropical Centre.**

(16) **Pass the I Wish Statue at the intersection of the two main pathways in the Middle Garden.** This sculpture of a little

girl's head was donated in 1946 by Leo Buring of Australian wine fame and fortune. It was sculpted by Arthur Fleischmann and is situated on the spot of the Botanic Gardens' original Wishing Tree. This special tree was planted in the Gardens in 1816. The tradition goes that children and lovers must walk around the Wishing Tree six times — three times forward and three times backwards — and then make a wish.

(17) **Pass the First Farm Display** where you can see exactly what and where the First Fleet planted. There is no other country in the world that can peg the exact site of its first garden. The First Fleet brought a large range of seeds to grow produce such as wheat, sugar cane, rice, coffee and cocoa, but the soil was poor and the farm was abandoned and moved to Parramatta after only six months.

(18) **The Tropical Centre has two enormous glasshouses —** The Arc and The Pyramid. The Arc

houses rare and unusual tropical plants from outside Australia. It has a special fogging system to simulate the environment of the cool and misty conditions of the high altitude tropics. The Pyramid houses northern Australian monsoonal woodland plants and tropical species from the rainforests along the north eastern Queensland coast and ranges.

(19) Though you can't see much evidence of the Garden Palace now, this land was once covered by an immense 244 metre long building that housed the 1879-80 Great International Exhibition. More than one million people went to see the Agricultural Trade Fair that promoted everything from food, wine and animals to sugar, wool and machinery. The Garden Palace was burnt to the ground in 1882 and arson was suspected. Convict ancestory records from the 1881 census were stored in the basement and rumour had it that someone torched the palace to destroy forever the shameful documents associated with being a convict.

(20) **Walk up the stairs and follow the signs to the Rose Garden,** where Noisette, China, Bourbon and Tea Roses are planted next to fabulous colour sequences of the modern rose species.

(21) **Walk through the Rose Garden Gate, in front of the Conservatorium of Music.** This building was originally designed as the stables to match Government House and as such became known as Governor Macquarie's 'folly'. He wanted a castellated-style stable, so architect Francis Greenway obliged. The stables became the Conservatorium of Music in 1915.

(22) **Go through the Government House gates and follow the sweeping driveway.** Access to Government House is a recent treat. Until January 1997 only VIPs were allowed to visit this 1845 Gothic Revivial building. The newly elected Labor government decided 'to return the building to the people'. The decision meant the New South Wales Governor would live in his own private home and visit Government House to perform his duties. Generally, the move was popular, but it was also criticised as 'republicanism by stealth'. An estimated 20,000 monarchists, the biggest non-union march this state has ever seen, marched in protest.

A roadway outside the gates and to the east of the grounds of the house leads you back around to the Opera House forecourt.

WALK 2

THE CITY ART WALK OF MUSEUMS AND GALLLERIES

START POINT:	Town Hall.
FINISH:	Hyde Park.
HOW TO GET THERE:	Trains from every direction in Sydney link up with Town Hall station — in the heart of Sydney's Central Business District.
LENGTH:	About 2 kilometres.
WALKING TIME:	1 hour.
ACTUAL TIME:	The whole day if you go inside the galleries and museums.
RATING:	Easy: the stroll is level and not physically demanding.
WEATHER CHECK:	This is a terrific rainy day walk.
REFRESHMENTS:	Each building has a coffee shop or restaurant.
	Suitable for wheelchairs and strollers: The galleries and museums all have wheelchair access.

*i*f you like art, relics and tales of early convict discipline, this walk should be one of your first choices. Some of Sydney's most important early colonial landmarks are covered in a short city loop. The Australian Museum, then elegant St Mary's Cathedral and onto the New South Wales Art Gallery. By cutting through a green mid-city park called the Domain, and going around the corner to New South Wales Parliament House, you'll find yourself at the old Mint Museum. Hyde Park Barracks with its grisly tales of convict floggings is next door. Then it's across Macquarie Street to a historic cluster of buildings that includes the Supreme and St James courthouses. Extensive historical information can be found at all these locations. This walk is designed to introduce you to the centre of Sydney, by covering some of its most important destinations.

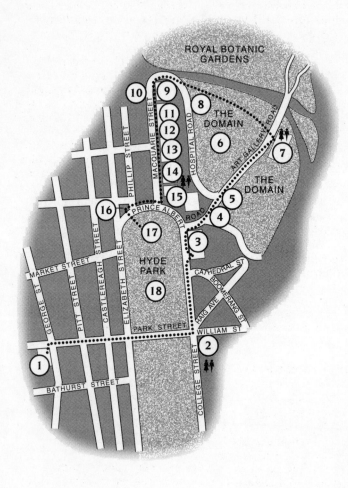

POINTS OF INTEREST ALONG THE WAY

(1) **Your start point is the Sydney Town Hall,** the site of Sydney's old burial ground. The first bodies were buried here five years after the First Fleet arrived. By 1820 the graveyard was full and by 1869 the coffins had to be moved to a Surry Hills graveyard. By then the Duke of Edinburgh had already laid the foundation stone for the Town Hall, and its facade was completed by the end of that year.

(2) **Leave the Town Hall and head up Park Street to College Street.** On the right-hand corner of the Park, opposite the Museum, you'll see a large statue of Captain Cook, the father of European settlement. Across the road is the Australian Museum, now one of the top five natural history museums in the world.

(3) **Come out of the Museum and head down College**

In the early 1800s hundreds of new Australian plant and animal species were being discovered and named. Explorers returned from expeditions with curious birds, shells, insects and reptiles—private collectors couldn't get enough of them and Europe was spellbound. A Londoner convicted of stealing clothes was the museum's first field collector and taxidermist.

Street. St Mary's Cathedral is in front of you — notice the two front towers; they should have spires, but they were never built because of a lack of money. St Mary's was designed by William Wardell. Construction began in 1866, but it wasn't until 1997 that the state government started a $5 million fund to add the spires. The Catholic church is trying to raise a further $3 million. Inside, the six altars are all made from New Zealand Oamaru stone. Check out the replica of Michelangelo's La Pieta—one of only four outside Italy. The Cathedral is made from Sydney sandstone, quarried at nearby Pyrmont.

(4) **Continue down College Street and turn right into Prince Albert Road, then left into Art Gallery Road,** past the Frazer Fountain in the middle of the intersection — it's one of several city fountains donated by rich Sydney merchant John Frazer in the 1880s. On your left is the impressive sandstone rear of the Lands Title Office.

(5) **Pass St Mary's Lodge,** and its sandstone gateposts erected more than 120 years ago when gates were needed to mark the entrance to the Domain Park. Built in 1835, the Lodge beside the old posts guarded a 34 hectare enclosed garden that was

> *More than 100 years ago, thousands of Irish Catholics who lived in the nearby dockside community of Wolloomooloo would walk up to St Mary's Cathedral for their Sunday worship. St Mary's Cathedral is built on the site of the first land grant to the Catholic church in Australia.*
>
> *At the time of writing, the area in front of the Cathedral was approved for a $30 million square that includes a tree-lined park and aquatic centre.*

only open on weekends. From 1860 the Domain stayed open at night and became known as 'The Park where the gates never close'.

(6) The Domain was formally established in 1792 when Governor Phillip set aside this point east of Sydney Cove as a reserve 'for the Crown and for the use of the Town of Sydney'. This grassy glade has a cricket tradition that dates back to the first representative match between England and New South Wales, played here in 1862. About a decade later the pitch was moved to the newly established Sydney Cricket Ground.

(7) You will soon come to the Art Gallery of New South Wales on your right. The first gallery on this site opened in 1885. It was an ugly, bare brick, windowless structure that was referred to as the 'art barn'. Then in 1895 Colonial Architect W.L.Vernon submitted the design

for the magnificent facade that you see now. Formally established in 1874 with 500 pounds, the money was given to a selection committee in London. At first the five trustees mainly invested in British Victorian and European art. But a tradition to commission local artists began shortly afterwards and by the 1920s Australian colonial art was being appreciated, and acquired. The first exhibitions date back to 1876. Various wings and picture galleries have been added over the years to provide for the Australian, European, Asian, Aboriginal and Melanesian collections inside.

(8) Leave the Art Gallery by the front entrance and choose the path across the road just off to the right through the Domain

> *Lachlan Macquarie came to Australia in 1810 and was known as a liberal with great vision for the colony. Macquarie held office for 11 years and the population tripled while under his care. His resignation was prompted by the Bigge Report into the state of the colony that found he was spending too much money on building projects. It appears he fell out of favour back in England because he was also encouraging too many convicts to become respectable citizens. Macquarie offered pardons as a reward for hard work—which diminished the colony's supply of forced labour.*

Park. This green field is also famous for the public speakers who stood on their soap boxes and aired their opinions, grievances or thoughts on the controversial topics of the day — much like London's Hyde Park. It started in the late 19th century but is rarely, if ever, practised now. You're walking towards the rear of the modern New South Wales Parliament House. The 12-storey office block, with 5 floors underground, was added in 1975 to the original 1816 building, which you'll see when you walk around Hospital Road.

⑨ On your left is the State Library of New South Wales, which is connected to the Mitchell Library. David Scott Mitchell devoted his life to tracking down and collecting early colonial manuscripts and rare Australiana. He bequeathed about 3000 items to the government — on the condition a building was provided to house them. These walls also house Captain Cook's diaries.

⑩ You are now on Macquarie Street, named after the fifth Governor of this state, Lachlan Macquarie. In the 1840s this thoroughfare was a fine residential address. 'Gentlemen's residences' and exclusive clubs blossomed, but as the traffic increased, the people moved out. Doctors associated with nearby Sydney Hospital moved in and by 1928 almost 400 members of the medical profession had surgeries here — Macquarie Street is still famous for its specialist doctors.

(11) **Parliament House** was built in 1816 as the home of the Rum Hospital's Principal Surgeon. Since 1856 New South Welshmen have regularly elected 99 members to the Legislative Assembly, or Lower House, to represent their area of the state. There are 42 members of the Legislative Council, or Upper House. They represent the whole state, and 21 members of the Legislative Council are elected every 4 years.

(12) **Outside Sydney Hospital** is the Wild Boar, Il Porcellino — give its nose a rub and make a wish. The Boar has a twin sister in Florence and was donated by a Florentine woman whose brother and father worked as surgeons in this hospital. Nurse training in Australia began here in 1868 when Florence Nightingale sent out 6 English sisters to establish a nursing school.

(13) **Parliament House, Sydney Hospital and The Mint** were all originally part of the huge Rum Hospital. The three buildings were constructed from 1816 to replace the makeshift hospital down the road at The Rocks. Builders were paid with a permit to import 45,000 gallons (or

205,000 litres) of rum. Alcohol, or permission to import and sell it, was as good as gold. Parliament and The Mint are twins; the hospital in the middle had to be demolished when it became unsafe.

(14) **The Mint** was built to house the Rum Hospital's Assistant Surgeon. Money was made here from 1853 to 1927. Inside is a fascinating collection of trophies from that era and earlier centuries.

(15) **For 29 years the Hyde Park Barracks** was a place of punishment. It was primarily a gaol from 1819 to 1848, but it also accommodated the chain gangs who worked outside for free men. Construction began without permission from the 'mother country', as England was spending

---

The Barracks housed about 1000 felons, despite originally being built to accommodate 600. By the year 1820, 25,000 convicts had been transported to Sydney. Over the following 30 years a further 120,000 arrived. Most of them were thieves, pickpockets and shoplifters. The average punishment for disobedience was 50 lashes per person. Scourgers (or floggers) used the cat-o-nine tails. Pink-skinned Englishmen who screamed after only a few lashes were known as sandstones because they crumbled so easily. It's said the ghosts of some of these men roam the Barracks.

Some of the games played at Hyde Park turned into blood sport when a group of early colonials organised two groups of Aborigines to fight each other with clubs and spears. Regular bets were laid and the fights continued until one of the Aboriginal warriors died from his wounds.

most of her money on the war against Napoleon. Macquarie hired a talented convict architect called Francis Greenway to design it. Greenway was transported for 14 years for forging a contract to get himself out of debt and Macquarie made good use of his talents.

16 Across the road is the New South Wales Supreme Court's modern 'piazza', called Queen's Square after the statue of Queen Victoria that looks down on it. Originally it was called Chancery Square, and was where the St James Church and courthouse attracted speakers to public meetings. Francis Greenway designed both and the little town square was completed in 1822.

17 The Archibald Fountain was bequeathed in 1927 to the citizens of Sydney by J.F. Archibald, founding editor of the *Bulletin* magazine. It commemorates the alliance between France and Australia during World War 1. It is regarded as the masterwork of its sculptor, Francois Sicard.

18 From 1810 to the late 1820s Hyde Park was a racetrack, its grandstand opposite David Jones department store. Australians have always loved a good bet and the 10 furlong course founded the NSW and Queensland tradition of racing clockwise. All sorts of sporting activities followed—wrestling, boxing, even a zoo complete with elephants, bears and a tiger was established here in 1849. In those days Hyde Park resembled something of a 'sideshow alley' during public holidays.

The Opera House and The Rocks Walks complete the heritage and history of many of the areas mentioned in the Art Walk.

THE
SHOPPING
WALK

START POINT:	The Queen Victoria Building.
FINISH:	Pitt Street.
HOW TO GET THERE:	Catch the train to Town Hall and exit via the signs for the QVB.
LENGTH:	The walk is only about 2 kilometres — it's up to you how you stretch it out.
WALKING TIME:	1 hour.
ACTUAL TIME:	At least a morning or an afternoon.
RATING:	Easy.
WEATHER CHECK:	This is an excellent rainy day walk.
REFRESHMENTS:	You'll pass dozens of cafes and restaurants.

Unsuitable for wheelchairs and strollers.

*t*here wouldn't be a traveller in the world that hasn't been frustrated by not knowing exactly where to go to find the best shops in an unknown city. This walk is a shopping expedition that links up the city's arcades and malls, so that you don't wander aimlessly around Sydney hoping that good luck will land you in front of just the kind of shop you were looking for. Walkers can crisscross the roads to their heart's content, but if you stick to the basic route set out for you, most of the city's best shops and boutiques will be covered. The walk starts at the Queen Victoria Building and finishes at the Piccadilly Arcade. In-between you'll walk through dozens of arcades that contain countless shops. The best Australian designers are there, along with the ritzy imported labels that spell expensive chic. History dots your path, and in the middle of your shopping blitz is Centrepoint's Sydney Tower, which offers the best view in town.

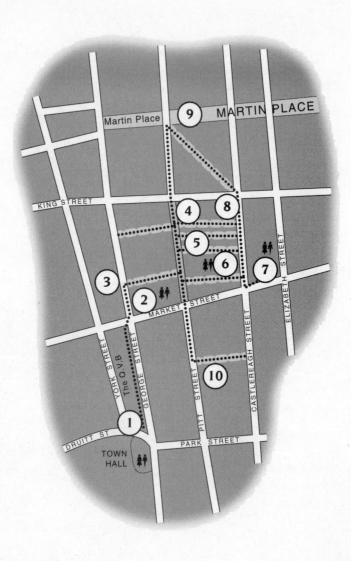

POINTS OF INTEREST ALONG THE WAY

① **The Queen Victoria Building** site was Sydney's early colonial marketplace. From 1810, the merchants here sold everything from pigs to vegetables to tools and clothing. Convicts were put into stocks in the middle of the market, a public humiliation for petty crimes. The present building was built from 1883 and has been restored many times since then. The QVB has one central copper dome and 20 smaller ones.

② **Leave the QVB from the Market Street exit and cross George Street**. The Grace Brothers department store should be on your right, followed by Dymocks Book Store — check out the Dymocks Building entrance — built from 1928.

③ **Turn right into the Mid City Centre**. After you've explored it head for the Pitt Street Mall and turn left for the 112 metre Strand Arcade, the longest in Sydney. This beautiful 3 level link between George and Pitt Streets was built in 1891 and destroyed by fire in 1970, but its restoration closely resembles the original design.

④ **Come out of the Strand and into the Pitt Street Mall**

Sydney Tower is the tallest building in the Southern Hemisphere. The observation deck gives a 360 degree view of the land surrounding Sydney — west to the Blue Mountains, north to Terrigal and south to Wollongong. Fifty-six cables anchor the Tower to Centrepoint — each cable weighs 7 tonnes and is made of 235 strands of 7mm thick wire. If the wires were laid end to end, the line would stretch from here to Alice Springs.

again. Enter the Glasshouse Arcade in front of you. It connects with the Skygarden Arcade next door.

5 **Come out of the Skygarden onto the Pitt Street Mall to enter the next arcade, called the Imperial.**
   Once you've examined the shops on the various levels, head for the Gallery Level, which connects with Castlereagh Street.

6 **Turn right into Castlereagh Street to enter Centrepoint via the Market Street corner entrance.** The escalators near this entrance take you to the Observation Level where you can catch the lift to the top of Sydney Tower. The elevator ride climbs 308 metres in 40 seconds.

7 **Leave Centrepoint and cross Castlereagh Street for the David Jones department store.**

(8) **Exit David Jones onto Castlereagh Street and head north** for a corner full of exclusive shops like Louis Vuitton, Chanel, Celine, Moschino and Gucci. They are all centred around the MLC, which we'll enter via the corner of King and Castlereagh streets. Walk through the MLC and exit following the Martin Place signs.

(9) **Martin Place** was initially proposed in 1888 to give the city an Italian-style piazza. But it wasn't until 1960 that Clarke Gazzard's idea to cut off the lower section of Martin Place for a civic square was taken seriously. The entire car-free Place was eventually completed in 1977 and some of the city's finest architecture surrounds it.

(10) **Turn left for Pitt Street, once again connecting with the mall which leads you up to Market Street. Continue up Pitt Street** for the final arcade in the walk — the Piccadilly Arcade, which has connections to David Jones on the ground floor and first floor.

WALK 4

KINGS CROSS TO ELIZABETH BAY

START POINT:	Kings Cross station.
FINISH:	Corner of Darlinghurst Road and Victoria Street, Kings Cross.
HOW TO GET THERE:	Catch the Eastern Suburbs train to Kings Cross station.
LENGTH:	Almost 4 kilometres.
WALKING TIME:	2 hours.
ACTUAL TIME:	Allow at least 2.5 hours.
RATING:	Easy: footpaths all the way with one uphill climb.
WEATHER CHECK:	Lots of shops and cafes to pop into should rain hamper your stroll.
REFRESHMENTS:	Takeaway food shops and cafes open all day. Kings Cross Markets are open every Sunday morning from 9 am.

Unsuitable for wheelchairs and strollers. This walk is recommended for daylight hours only.

*e*very city has its red light district — Sydney has Kings Cross. It's colourful, sleazy and sleepless, with a fascinating history. This arm of land was probably Australia's first official Aboriginal Reserve. Governor Lachlan Macquarie (1810-22) called the area Henrietta Town, and it was also known as Blacktown. The Aborigines were dying, so Macquarie had huts built so they might 'live peaceably and industriously'. But one year after Macquarie left Sydney, Blacktown was given over for others to use. Governor Ralph Darling (1825-31) decided the colony needed a region exclusively for the wealthy. He chose Blacktown because of its stupendous views of the harbour, called it Woolloomooloo Heights and carved it up. By 1831, 17 rich public servants, Sydney's most powerful men, were building their grand houses along this ridge. The walk takes you to some of these homes and tells you of their owner's history. In 1850 the area was subdivided. New streets were mapped out for the elegant terraces of businessmen and merchants and 20 years later the first of the big mansions began to disappear as high density living exploded and the country's first apartment blocks were needed. Kings Cross, Potts Point and Elizabeth Bay were born and became swank addresses. Come 1916, new laws forced pubs to close at 6 pm. In retaliation, the Cross became sly. Grog was peddled in the shadows and gangsters ruled. That's when the old Kings Cross Road became known as the 'Dirty Half Mile'. During the Second World War, American servicemen on leave came in search of a good time. They brought their hamburgers, club sandwiches and nylon stockings. Kings Cross provided the booze, women and entertainment.

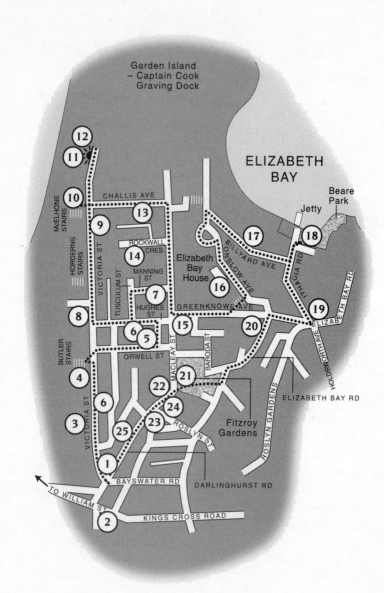

Garden Island
– Captain Cook
Graving Dock

ELIZABETH BAY

Beare Park

Jetty

McELHONE STAIRS

CHALLIS AVE

HORDERNS STAIRS

VICTORIA ST

ROCKWALL CRES.

TUSCULUM ST

MANNING ST

Elizabeth Bay House

BILLYARD AVE

ONSLOW AVE

ITHACA RD

HUGHES ST

GREENKNOWE AVE

BUTLER STAIRS

ORWELL ST

MACLEAY ST

BARODA ST

ELIZABETH BAY RD

VICTORIA ST

ROSLYN GARDENS

ELIZABETH BAY RD

Fitzroy Gardens

ROSLYN ST

TO WILLIAM ST

BAYSWATER RD

DARLINGHURST RD

KINGS CROSS ROAD

HOLDSWORTH AVE

ELIZABETH BAY RD

POINTS OF INTEREST ALONG THE WAY

(1) Take the William Street exit from Kings Cross station and turn right. You'll soon see the Coca-Cola sign at the intersection of William Street, Victoria Street and Kings Cross Road. Stand on the corner of Victoria Street. William Street was a dirt track until the late 1830s, with the only access east through South Head Road (now Oxford Street). This area, eventually known as the 'Top of the Cross', has always suffered chronic traffic chaos. Early land grants with magnificent homes forced the construction of William Street to stop abruptly here. In 1916 the local council widened the thoroughfare by bulldozing almost 100 properties down William Street's south side. A further attempt to ease congestion saw the Kings Cross tunnel completed in 1975, but traffic is still bumper-to-bumper on Friday and Saturday nights.

(2) The suburb of Darlinghurst starts beyond the Coke sign, where you can see the charming old 1910 Darlinghurst Fire Station on the corner. It's still in use. Darlinghurst was named after New South Wales Governor Sir Ralph Darling — 'hurst' comes from the English word meaning 'woods'.

(3) Turn right and head North up Victoria Street. We can thank Judge James Dowling for the wideness of Victoria Street, as extra space for roads was gained when he donated some of his estate. His land was subdivided in 1846. Many of Victoria Street's terraces appeared between 1870 and 1890. Victoria Street is listed under the National Heritage Trust.

(4) About 400 metres down Victoria Street on the left are the sandstone pillars of the Butler Stairs where you'll see a memorial plaque to Mick Fowler, who spearheaded the fight against the high-rise developers.

(5) Turn right up Orwell Street, almost opposite the steps,

Victoria Street has developed into a backpackers' paradise, but it has a murderous history. In 1971 developers wanted to demolish 32 houses on its western side. In protest, local residents joined forces with the Builders' Labourers' Federation, and Green Bans forbidding demolition work were placed on the houses. In 1975 campaigner, journalist and heiress to the Mark Foys fortune, Juanita Nielson, disappeared. The developers, unions and residents eventually reached a compromise after a long and often violent battle, and most of the houses were retained. Juanita's body was never found.

and pass **Springfield Gardens. On your left soon is the Metro Theatre,** which used to be the Minerva Theatre. Some of Australia's most well-known wartime actors, such as Peter Finch and Ron Randell, cut their teeth here. In the late 1970s the Metro was bought by *Mad Max* producers Kennedy-Miller Entertainments. Much of the TV mini-series *The Dismissal* was filmed here.

(6) Turn left into Macleay Street and immediately left again into Hughes Street. Halfway down on your left is the Wayside Chapel, founded in 1964 by the Reverend Ted Noffs. This is Christian outreach at its best. In an area renowned for its vice, counselling and help is available here 24 hours a day. Ted Noffs, known as 'The Man of the Cross', changed many hearts for the better.

(7) To see one of the villas that remains, turn right into Tusculum Street, then right into Manning Street. One of the most popular architects of these 1830s' grand houses was John Verge. No. 3 Manning Street shows his style. This is one of the finest early colonial regency mansions left in Australia. Designed and built in 1831, the cedar panelling that you can see on the outside ceilings was imported from Lebanon. Inside, its marble floor and chimneypieces were imported from Italy. The original owner went bankrupt in the 1840s'

In the 1920s and 1930s most of the villas on the early land grants were destroyed. Hughes Street is a great example of the apartment blocks that replaced them. By the end of the Thirties Kings Cross was the most densely populated area in Australia.

Depression and sold the house to liquor merchant William Long. It was rumoured the Long family slept with police rattles and lined every window with hanging alarm bells for fear of intruders.

(8) Double back into Hughes Street and turn right for Victoria Street again, where you're faced with the elegant sandstone villa at No. 113 and the Italianate terrace at No. 111.

(9) Soon you'll pass the stone wall of St Vincent's College on your right. This school is the result of a remarkable expedition from Ireland in 1838 by five Sisters of Charity. They came with a black Jesus Christ nailed to a weighty iron cross because they'd heard the natives here were black. They set up the first St Vincent's Hospital on this site in 1857, which grew into the present school. St Vincent's Hospital is now located in nearby Darlinghurst.

(10) The McElhone Steps are where the cityside terraces end, on the left of Victoria Street. These steps replaced wooden ladders, which before the 1830s were the only way to get

down to Woolloomooloo Bay or up to Woolloomooloo Heights. Now they let the walker access the city via the coast, and the Domain within half an hour.

⑪ Move along a few metres to the concrete lookout for a glorious view of Woolloomooloo Bay and Cowper Wharf. Once a sleepy bay of green farmland with extensive muddy flats at low tide, this area was granted to John Palmer only five years after he arrived with the First Fleet. From 1840 workers built their cottages here so they could be close to town. In the 1860s, wharfage, with all its associated vices such as blackmarket profiteering and prostitution, boomed. The bay's murderous razor gangs and sly grog distillers spilled up into the Cross until the late 1920s. By the 20th century the old grey wharf in front of you had become a major passenger terminal. It's no longer in use, but hundreds of navy vessels dock annually at Garden Island's defence dock directly below you.

> *The first white settlers recorded that this bay was a favourite place of the Cadigal tribe. They often gathered here and referred to it as 'wallah mullah' or 'wallah', which could have various meanings — 'resting place for the dead', 'young male kangaroo' or 'place of plenty'. The real meaning is unknown.*

⑫ Where you now stand is Potts Point, first called

Caragheen, then Paddy's Point. Following an ownership dispute over a land grant, it was finally named Potts Point after Joseph Potts, an 1829 New South Wales Bank (now Westpac) official. Until 1940 the land to your extreme right did not exist. Water separated the point from a shady outcrop called Garden Island — an island that resembled a lovely garden. In the Second World War Australia's allies needed somewhere to service their ships while fighting in the Pacific, so 13 hectares between the point and the island were filled in to build the huge Garden Island Graving Dock.

⑬ Cross Victoria Street and head up Challis Avenue, a classic street of late 19th and early 20th century houses. Nos. 21 and 23 were built in the late Victorian period and are Classical Revival style. Nos. 25 and 27 are in Romanesque style: notice the elaborately moulded ground floor colonnade and delicate cast-iron upper verandah balustrades.

⑭ Turn right into Macleay Street. Rockwall Crescent is almost immediately on your right. Stand on the corner to admire another stately home designed by John Verge — Rockwall — just down Rockwall Crescent on the left. It was built in 1830 for John Busby, the civil engineer responsible for identifying Sydney's second water source, Busby's Bore (see the Centennial Park Walk). John Busby became known as a snobbish and difficult man to work with. He was ultimately nicknamed Busby the Bore.

(15) **Cross Macleay Street and turn left down Greenknowe Avenue.** The corner block at No. 1 Greenknowe Avenue is the eight-storey apartment building Kingsclere, reportedly Sydney's first block of units. It was designed by architects Halligam and Wilton in 1912 and heralded the beginning of a succession of grand 'flats'. Many were serviced by full-time servants and restaurants. Kings Cross's oldest residents recall Kingsclere had a rooftop cinema. The affluent lifestyle of Kingsclere came to an end with the beginning of the First World War. Continue down Greenknowe Avenue and you're in Elizabeth Bay, named after Governor Macquarie's wife, Elizabeth Henrietta Campbell.

(16) **Turn left down Onslow Avenue and follow the signs to Elizabeth Bay House.** Elizabeth Bay House was restored to look almost exactly as it did in 1839-45, when it housed New South Wales Colonial Secretary Alexander Macleay and his family. He was second in charge after the governor, so his perfectly positioned land grant was the best — the house was famous as the finest in the colony. Macleay had a passion for plants. The house was renowned for its glorious garden of native and imported plants from China, Brazil and the West Indies. The Macleay family sold Elizabeth Bay House in 1911 and for many years it was derelict. In 1940 it was converted into 16 flats. It is now a part of the Historic Houses Trust.

(17) **Turn left upon exiting Elizabeth Bay House and right at the bottom of the hill into Billyard Avenue,** lined with some of Sydney's choicest real estate. No. 42 is Boomerang, built in 1926 for music millionaire Frank Albert. He made his fortune through Boomerang sheet music and mouth organs. Later the Albert family owned radio stations and financed movies, such as *Strictly Ballroom*.

(18) **Beares Park fronts the harbour at the end of Billyard Avenue.** During the war years boys would store rowing boats here, which they used to collect sailors from nearby naval ships and bring them into the Cross for the cost of a shilling. The cast-iron drinking fountain dates back to 1857.

(19) **Walk up Ithaca Road to where it intersects with Roslyn Gardens and Elizabeth Bay Road**. On another day turn down Holdworth Avenue for a

beautiful walk across historic Rushcutters Bay, through the Cruising Yacht Club's marina and up to Darling Point.

(20) At the intersection turn right up Elizabeth Bay Road and follow it left up the hill past the Sebel Town House Hotel. This road began as the driveway to Elizabeth Bay House.

(21) Soon a small mall is visible on your right; this is Fitzroy Gardens. An elaborate mansion called Maramanah occupied this area after the Macleay estate was subdivided. It was sold to the council in 1945 and demolished in 1954 to make way for this public park. Further into Fitzroy Gardens is the El Alamein Fountain, a Kings Cross landmark. Known by locals as the 'Dandelion Fountain', it commemorates the siege of Tobruk and the battle of El Alamein.

(22) Walk through Fitzroy Gardens to Darlinghurst Road, where it intersects with Macleay Street. Near here, at No. 17 Darlinghurst Road, was the home of David Scott Mitchell, the man at the centre of Sydney's Mitchell Library. Mitchell led a long and solitary life here with the books that formed the library's centrepiece. He tracked down and returned to Australia valuable manuscripts that had been taken back to Europe. He donated thousands of manuscripts, books and volumes to ensure Australia had a fine record

of early settlement. David Scott Mitchell lived to see the library's commemoration stone laid in 1906.

(23) On the corner of Roslyn Street is the ANZ Bank. It was once a block of apartments with an attic on top where the famous artist William Dobell lived and worked.

(24) On Roslyn Street's other corner is the old site of Les Girls. From 1963 to 1989 boys dressed up as beautiful girls and thrilled audiences with their cabaret shows full of risque humour and wisecracks. This club, as well as the fancy dress balls held at the famous Trocadero nightclub, were later seen as the forerunners to Sydney's enormously successful Gay and Lesbian Mardi Gras.

(25) Continue along Darlinghurst Road into the heart of the red light district, known in the early part of this century as 'the dirty half mile'.

You'll shortly find yourself outside Kings Cross station where your walk began.

In 1897 Kings Cross was known as Queens Cross, to commemorate Queen Victoria's reign. It became Kings Cross in honour of King Edward VII in 1905.

THE ROCKS

START POINT:	Circular Quay.
FINISH:	George Street, The Rocks.
HOW TO GET THERE:	Dozens of buses service Circular Quay, or catch the train to Wynyard and walk down George Street. The ideal way to reach the quay is by ferry.
LENGTH:	Almost 4 kilometres.
WALKING TIME:	1.5 hours.
ACTUAL TIME:	Definitely under 2 hours.
RATING:	Easy: the route weaves through old lanes and streets, with a paved incline up to Observatory Hill. The rest is all downhill.
WEATHER CHECK:	Loads of galleries, shops and cafes to rest or browse in should rain hamper your walk.
REFRESHMENTS:	Plenty of choice with cafes and restaurants. The Rocks market is open from 10 am on Saturday and Sunday.

A wheelchair access route is available from The Rocks Information Centre at 106 George Street.

*S*ituated underneath the Harbour Bridge and over-looking the Opera House, The Rocks is one of Australia's most beautifully preserved 19th century colonial villages. It has a special place in history because this is where Captain Arthur Phillip founded white Australia after Botany Bay proved too shallow. In January 1788 Phillip ordered the six convict ships, three store-ships and two navy vessels to Sydney Cove, where there was plenty of room for anchorage and precious water flowed from the Tank Stream. After eight months at sea, the 1030 people straggled onto dry land and England's furthest flung penal colony was established. Phillip sent the convicts to the cove's steep and rocky western shore. Hobbled in leg irons, they cleared land, raised tents and built huts for shelter. Gradually vegetable gardens, storerooms, a bakehouse and a hospital appeared as village life spread up the rocky cliffs of the cove. Life in the fledgling settlement was grim, and in The Rocks many of the social aspects of those years are preserved. This walk takes you around the earliest cottages and scariest alleyways. Fascinating characters and tales of their struggles to survive punctuate this easy amble around Australia's finest example of early colonial life.

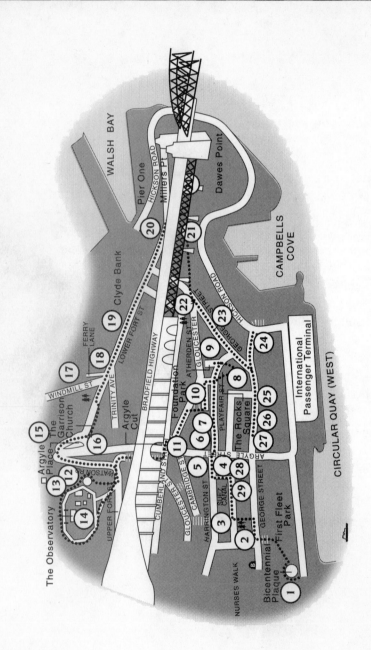

POINTS OF INTEREST ALONG THE WAY

(1) **At Circular Quay face the harbour, with the Opera House on your right. Turn left (west) and walk towards the First Fleet Park's bicentennial plaque on the ground in the corner. It gives a wonderful image of The Rocks as it was in the colony's earliest times. Walk up the stairs beside the Museum of Contemporary Art.** The geography here was totally different 200 years ago. Sydney Cove was an estuary that stretched 100 metres south back to Bridge Street and west up to where the museum's doorstep now stands. Semi-Circular Quay construction started in 1837.

The Tank Stream that still flows underground here was initially called the Spring Stream. But the tanks and wells that soon dotted its banks resulted in a name change. It took only seven years of settlement to partially foul the stream. Householders used it as a dumping ground for sewage and garbage. In 1795 a new law threatened to pull down any houses where pigs were allowed to roam through open palings and further foul the Tank Stream. Offenders were also forced to donate 5 pounds to the Orphans' Fund. Twenty-five years later the Tank Stream was putrid. By 1840 thousands of convicts had filled it in to form the seawall that you can see now.

Convicts lugged stones and boulders from the nearby Argyle Cut and Fort Denison to fill in almost 5 hectares of a muddy, sandy beach. The wharf was completed seven years later. There have been many changes since then and the name has been shortened to Circular Quay.

(2) **You are now on Lower George Street.** At No. 143 in front of you is the Russell Hotel — notice the shingled roof and tower. No. 135 is an old bank, built in 1886. Further on is the original police station, where the old lockup cells are almost as they were when built in 1882. The police station closed in 1974 — wander in and have a look.

(3) **Walk underneath the archway next door to the old police station. Follow the signs to the Nurses' Walk**, and Surgeons' Court, so called because this is the site where the First Fleet set up their portable hospital. The two makeshift structures were staffed by unpaid convicts. The Second Fleet brought another portable hospital, which was ready by 1790. Within weeks almost 500 patients spilled over into tents, pitched to care for the overflow. The Nurses' Walk was created by the Sydney Cove Authority to connect with the 'Suez Canal'.

thoroughfare was favoured by prostitutes and thugs.

(5) Turn right into Harrington Street, where almost immediately you'll come across the old Reynolds Cottage on your right at No. 30. This is where William Reynolds, his wife and two children lived. Reynolds arrived from Dublin in 1817 on a life sentence. In the 1830s he built several small cottages here, though Nos. 28 and 30 were built around 1823. An excavation of the backyard where Reynolds ran his blacksmith shop revealed evidence of cock-fighting and dog-baiting (in which he used *live* cats). Wander in and have a look at No. 28. These cottages are two classic examples of the one room upstairs and one room downstairs early home design. They've been restored using the original construction methods.

(4) The Nurses' Walk veers right, past the site of the first bakehouse, then left up the 'Suez Canal'. The earliest reference to this alley is on an 1805 map when it was called Cornwell Lane. Understandably nicknamed the Sewer's Canal, this narrow passageway was once an open sewer through which effluent flowed. It was eventually filled in, but throughout the 1800s this

In 1900 the bubonic plague struck Sydney: 103 people died and 303 contracted the disease. Overcrowding meant that on average 35 people used one toilet. As a result of the plague, health inspectors declared some of The Rocks uninhabitable. The government resumed houses and land and demolished the contaminated and dilapidated slums, open sewers and outhouses.

(6) Cross Argyle Street into Playfair Street, with the Argyle Arts Centre on your left. Originally this area was dedicated to the vegetable garden that fed the nearby hospital. Native herbs and exotic plants were grown to relieve the shortage of drugs. Then, in 1826, Captain John Piper started to build his house, but never finished it. The Argyle Bond Store opened here in the same year. Warehouses were added after Mary Reiby bought the store and sold it to several people. The rear section dates from 1840. Over the following 80 years another 17 parts were added.

> Born in 1777, Mary Reiby was 13 years old when she stole a horse as a practical joke and was sentenced to seven years' transportation. She married a successful businessman at 17, who died 17 years later. Mary, the mother of seven, expanded her businesses, bought many properties and became one of Sydney's most respected and admired women.

(7) Next door is the Argyle Terrace. This area was first used by Michael Cross, a dairyman who grazed his cows alongside the vegetable garden. In 1875 several affluent men built these houses and called them Tara Terrace. In those days the houses were rented by a shipwright, a coppersmith and blacksmith, a printer, a draughtsman and a master mariner.

(8) Continue towards The Rocks Square to the sandstone statue by Bud Dumas called 'First Impressions'. It reflects the three dimensions of early colonial life — the convicts, the military and the free settlers.

(9) Next to the statue is Sydney's tiniest street, Atherden Street. Whale oil was one of the most profitable exports in early colonial times and this is where Ben Boyd housed his successful whaling warehouse and business. The terraces numbered 1, 3, 5 and 7 were built in 1880 by Thomas Playfair, a Rocks butcher who became Mayor of Sydney. Nos. 6

and 8 were added the following year.

(10) Double back and turn right just before Argyle Terrace into the rocky terrain of Foundation Park. This area gives a fantastic example of how life in the 1800s adapted to living on a sandstone ridge. Walk up the stairs to see how the houses were cut into rock faces, the size of the workers' cottages obvious from what remains. Poverty forced about seven people to share one of those homes. These terraces were built between 1875 and 1877 and were demolished in 1938.

(11) At the top of the stairs turn left into Gloucester Walk, then climb the Argyle Steps, built in 1926, along with the Cumberland Street overpass. **Turn left and cross the Cumberland Street overpass.** This is the top of The Rocks ridge, were the affluent lived and built plush terraces before the Depression of the 1840s. By the turn of the century the area had degenerated into a slum. The land needed for the Harbour Bridge pylons took many of the houses that the 1900 plague demolitions had left behind.

(12) Continue through the Harbour Bridge pylon lookout entrance called 'Bridge Stairs' and take the Fort Street exit. Turn left and head for the Rotunda. This part of the walk takes you up to Observatory Hill, where you can set your bearings.

In front of the overpass is the famous Argyle Cut. There was no access to Millers Point from The Rocks other than steep stairways, so work began on this tunnel in 1843. Convict chain gangs attacked the sandstone with picks and hammers. It took 24 years to complete. The Cut was a place to be feared when the infamous Push Gangs hung out here from the 1870s. This subculture was at first mischievous and cheeky, but turned vicious when gangs also developed at Kings Cross and Woolloomooloo. They often clashed with the Argyle Cut Push, who in turn fought against The Rocks Push. The era closed with the 1900 plague.

Across the harbour is North Sydney and further west is the Parramatta River. Immediately west is the beginning of Darling Harbour, with the container terminals of White Bay and Johnstons Bay and the Glebe Island Bridge. The 87 metre high concrete tower is the Port Operations and Communications Centre which keeps a watch over harbour shipping movements, oil spillages and maritime accidents.

(13) The views from Observatory Hill were first used for an 1803 fort, and its walls still surround the observatory. There was constant fear the thousands of convicts might rebel or that the French would attack the new British colony. In 1825 a signal station was built on the hillside facing The Rocks. Flags were raised here and at the signal station on South Head to send messages to and fro.

(14) Behind the Rotunda is the Sydney Observatory, which began as a time ball tower. The ball above the observatory's wall was ordered from England in the 1850s — every day it would drop at exactly 1 pm to let the people of Sydney know the time. BOOM! A cannon was fired simultaneously from Fort Denison. Construction of the observatory followed in 1858. Another observatory, at Parramatta, had already documented 7385 previously unknown stars by 1835. **Walk around the observatory to the entrance to see the gardens and Fort Phillip wall.**

(15) Leave the observatory and head downhill to Argyle Place. Governor Lachlan Macquarie christened Argyle Place after his birthplace in Scotland. At the west end you can see the 1842 Lord Nelson Hotel, the oldest pub in Sydney.

(16) Walk towards the Garrison Church. Imagine the redcoats of the 50th Regiment marching here from the Dawes Point Battery down the road. They would come every day for morning service. This Holy Trinity Church was the first garrison church in Australia; its foundation stone was laid in 1840.

(17) Head down Lower Fort Street and pass Windmill Street with its corner pub — the

Hero of Waterloo Hotel. Stories of shanghaied sailors stem from this old drinking spot. When drunken men passed out at the bar, the barmen would spirit them away through underground tunnels to waiting ships in need of crewmen.

(18) **The next corner is Ferry Lane,** where Sydney's first case of the bubonic plague was isolated at No. 10. Poor Arthur Payne. His clean and tidy house

In the 1970s the government launched a Rocks Redevelopment Plan that would have seen these houses demolished. Thanks to the resident at No. 35 George Street, the government was never to realise their high-rise plans. Nita McCrae led The Rocks Residents' Group to the Builders' Labourers' Federation. The union placed Green Bans on the homes and no work proceeded. The developers finally backed off and The Rocks was saved.

puzzled the health inspectors at first, until they discovered a disgusting sewerage system that obviously hadn't worked for some time. Payne and all his Lower Fort and Kent Street neighbours were carted off to the Quarantine Station by 26 January 1900. Much of Millers Point was demolished after the discovery.

(19) **At No. 43 Lower Fort Street is Clyde Bank, the city's oldest home.** Robert Crawford completed this house in 1825 after he was given a land grant in 1823 by his good friend Governor Brisbane. Brisbane also gave him a good job as Principal Clerk to the Colonial Secretary, so Crawford's home was only a ten minute walk from his office. Clyde Bank was renamed Bligh House by the younger Robert Campbell, the son of super-rich merchant Robert Campbell, who bought it in 1833. The property was restored in 1963.

(20) The west side of this point is called Millers Point because Jack the Miller — or John Leighton — built Sydney's first windmills here to grind grain. The colony's early bread was known for its coarseness because the windmills worked in a stop-start fashion which resulted in a rough, uneven texture and therefore tough bread.

(21) Turn right (east) to walk underneath the bridge pylons to Dawes Point, where Australia's first astronomer, William Dawes, set up his stargazer lookout point. The young lieutenant arrived with the First Fleet. When he returned to England four years later, his observatory was turned into a guardhouse, later razed for the construction of the Harbour Bridge in 1925.

(22) You should now be back on George Street, first called Sergeant Majors Row. Nos. 25 to 27 is The Mercantile Hotel, built in 1914 for Tooth and Company Ltd.

(23) Next door is a row of old homes, beginning with two sandstone dwellings at Nos. 29 and 30. William Reilly built them in 1866. They were passed on to a leather merchant who worked and lived here until the buildings were used as boarding houses from 1888. The five terraces at Nos. 33 to 41 were built in 1881. From 1885 they too were mainly used as boarding houses. No. 43 is the oldest terrace, with its narrow sandstone workshop next door. Built in 1848, the house and shop had various merchant owners until finally in 1870 Frederick Ward made and sold his soap powder, cordial and vinegar from here. On the opposite side of George Street are the Metcalf Bond Stores, built between 1812 and 1816.

(24) Turn left at the corner of Hickson Road and go to the stairs with the sign 'Campbells Storehouse'. Robert Campbell bought this waterfront land 11 years after the First Fleet arrived. He was the first merchant to own large warehouse and wharfage facilities. You can still see his ten storehouses, built by 1861. On another day you can walk around the foreshore underneath the Harbour Bridge.

(25) Continue along George Street past the old

One year after the First Fleet arrived, at least half the tribe of Aborigines that lived in this area were dead. The total of Sydney's Cadigal population has been guessed at many times. Records indicate there were at least 500 Aborigines up, down and around Sydney Cove. Their numbers were decimated by the 1789 smallpox epidemic. The rest were relegated to the outskirts of town, where they slowly died of other illnesses or starvation.

Maritime Church at No. 100 to the old Morgue and Coroner's Court at Nos. 102-104. The cases heard here have made many a hair stand on end, especially the gruesome Shark Arm Murder. In 1935, in a chance in a million, a shark caught off Coogee Beach vomited up a tattooed human arm. The 'good condition' of the arm meant the fingerprints were still present, and the arm was identified as that of missing man James Smith — SP bookmaker and small-time thief. A number of suspects were interviewed, but before charges could be laid, a key witness was murdered. The identity of the person who fed Smith to the sharks was never established. The courthouse was built in 1907 and still stands. It's now an antique store. The Morgue was demolished in 1972.

(26) **The Tourist Information Centre at No. 106 is definitely worth investigating.** The building used to be the Sydney Sailors' Home, dedicated to the welfare of 19th century sailors who needed somewhere cheap and clean to sleep. The north wing was completed in 1864.

(27) **Next is 110 George Street, Cadman's Cottage — the oldest surviving home in Sydney.** This two-storey dwelling was built on Sydney Cove's waterline in 1816 for the Government Coxswain. His job involved organising the 20 boats that transported officers and convicts to the colony's outlying areas. In those days waterways provided the only access west to important destinations such as Parramatta, via the river, and east to South Head. Privately owned boats were illegal for fear of convict escape. John Cadman was appointed boat superintendent in 1827. Cadman's Cottage now houses the National Parks and Wildlife Information Centre.

(28) **No. 91 George Street now belongs to the police.** From 1790 to 1816 the site belonged to the home and gardens of the Assistant Surgeons to the various ships that brought convicts to Sydney. Famous architect and convict Francis Greenway moved in until the 1830s. The building you see now was constructed in 1841.

Continue up George Street to Circular Quay, where your walk started.

CHINA TOWN TO DARLING HARBOUR

START POINT:	Town Hall.
FINISH:	Darling Harbour.
HOW TO GET THERE:	Trains from every direction in Sydney link up with Town Hall station — in the heart of Sydney's Central Business District.
LENGTH:	4 kilometres, though how you stretch out your stroll around Darling Harbour is up to you.
WALKING TIME:	2–3 hours.
ACTUAL TIME:	Definitely a day excursion, or at least the afternoon.
RATING:	Easy.
WEATHER CHECK:	This is an excellent rainy day walk.
REFRESHMENTS:	China Town and Darling Harbour are packed with restaurants.

Suitable for wheelchairs and strollers — though be prepared to do battle with pedestrians. Note: Paddy's Market is only open on weekends.

Sydney's China Town is a lively, vibrant Asian quarter that has all the sights, sounds and smells of Hong Kong — and the fabulous shopping that goes with it. Chinese emporiums, businesses and restaurants spill onto Dixon and Sussex streets, the street life busy with the kind of organised chaos that guarantees a great walk. Next door to the oriental neighbourhood is Paddy's Market, one of Sydney's oldest and biggest bargain hunter's playgrounds. China Town is also the gateway to one of the city's premier tourist destinations — Darling Harbour. This stroll is designed to cover the most interesting ground in the shortest distance. It's a guide that links the history and culture of China Town to Paddy's Market and Darling Harbour, so that visitors do not miss any 'must see' locations. With two museums, an aquarium, the world's largest movie screen, virtual reality games and a huge harbour park for water and sporting shows, we leave you at Darling Harbour — which has enough entertainment to keep everyone happy. It's also a major Olympic venue for Sydney's 2000 Games, where the boxing, judo and weightlifting competitions will be held. The route continues on to Sydney's new casino, or returns to the city via the old Pyrmont Bridge that is now a pedestrian link. More than anything Darling Harbour has a spirit of fun — this walk leads you to it, without forgetting how history moulded it into what it is today.

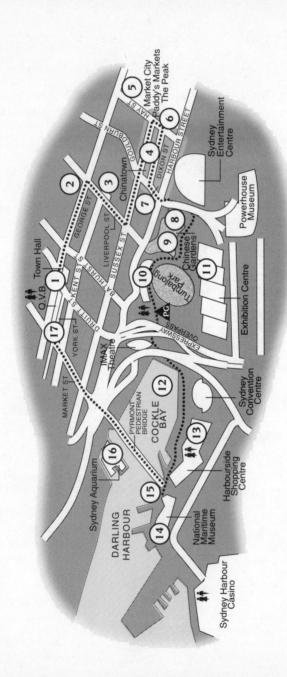

POINTS OF INTEREST ALONG THE WAY

(1) **With your back to the Town Hall, turn right and head through Sydney Square and down George Street past St Andrew's Cathedral.** Sydney's Town Hall was built on the site of a burial ground, in use till 1818. The land was farmed by a recluse called Tom Dick, but when he was murdered no-one claimed his property so it reverted to the state. The foundation stone for the Cathedral was laid in 1837. The finished work was designed by Edmund Blackett and completed in 1869.

> *You are now walking down Brickfield Hill, a once treacherously steep track where convicts dug clay so they could bake bricks for the colony's first buildings. In the early 1800s there was a little village here called Brickfield. In the 1830s the chaingangs began to level it making it more like the George Street you see today.*

(2) **Walk through 'cinema city', the centre of Sydney's movie district.** Turn right at Liverpool Street, where you'll soon come across a tiny Spanish quarter that's dotted with Latin-type restaurants, delis and clubs.

(3) **On your left you'll soon see The Waldorf apartment block,** which gives a perfect example of how the needs of industry and then tourism have changed the city's housing. An 1831 map of colonial Sydney records a little wooden dwelling here on the Waldorf site. By 1865 the home had become a large one-storey timber villa, with a wide verandah at the back. In 1890 a cul-de-sac was added to provide a sweeping driveway to mews and terraces that had been built in the villa's backyard. In 1928 the whole lot, including the cul-de-sac, was levelled for the Balfour building — an early office block made of red brick. Then in the early 1980s when tourism demanded more accommodation in the city, the Waldorf replaced the Balfour with 17 floors of apartments.

(4) **Turn left into Sussex Street — keep an eye out for the cobblestone laneway on your left that remains from the old cul-de-sac behind the Waldorf — and continue down to the Goulburn Street intersection where China Town really begins.** Australia's first Chinese businessmen mostly ran laundries, or boarding or gambling houses. Others cultivated and sold fruit and vegetables, while the very first merchants sold imported tea, rice, ginger, herbs, pottery, fabric and ceramics. This stretch of China Town has expanded from a small Asian enclave to a vibrant multi-million

Gold fever, the end of convict transportation and a demand for cheap labour brought thousands of Chinese to Australia in the 1850s. But by 1870 racism was on the increase in Australia and the Chinese bore the brunt of it, despite the fact that in 1892 a Royal Commission into Chinese gambling and immorality found that 'the Chinese are, apart from that disposition to gamble, a singularly peaceable and generally law abiding section of the community'. In 1901 a census showed there were 10,000 Chinese living in New South Wales — of that number, only 103 were women.

dollar shopping district, where the arcades that link Sussex Street with Dixon Street have a distinct upmarket Hong Kong fashion flavour.

5 **Continue down Sussex Street to Paddy's Market.** Stallholders in this huge warehouse have been pushed around Sydney for about 150 years. The markets originated up at the Queen Victoria Building's old George Street markets in 1830, while the first Paddy's Markets were built here between 1908 and 1911. They ultimately grew too big for the building and were moved out to Flemington. At one time Paddy's covered the whole area now occupied by the Entertainment Centre and the University of Technology Sydney. The market is now the cornerstone for Market City, which lies underneath the $300 million

Malaysian owned residential building, 'The Peak'.

6 **The 'light rail' tracks outside Paddy's** revives the spirit of Sydney's old trams, which were dumped in 1961. This smooth new version started operating in July 1997 and proved to be so successful the government added 2 extra routes to the original one at a cost of $230 million.

7 **After the market head up the Dixon Street Mall. Turn left at the end so that you're on the busy corner of Pier and Harbour streets** where John Dickson built his state-of-the-art steam driven windmill in 1815. This is how Dixon Street gained its name — Dickson increased the colony's grain production from 20 bushels a week to 960 with his steam windmill. He built a dam across the bay to harness the water for his steam.

8 **Cross Harbour Street and walk to the right of the Sydney Entertainment Centre to the Pump House Tavern,** built on the site of Australia's first steam engine. The hydraulic power was used to pump pressurised water through 80 kilometres of pipes under the city. The casings for the original accumulators and the deep water tank in the roof are still here and preserved under the National Trust.

9 **Continue walking to the right, under the highway passover, till you come to the**

Chinese Gardens. This serene city oasis was designed in the traditional southern Chinese style by landscape gardeners of the Guangdong Province. New South Wales and Guangdong are sister states and this garden commemorates the relationship. Inside the walls you'll find lotus covered lakes, waterfalls and tranquil pavilions surrounded by Chinese native plants.

This area was originally a long, flat, muddy beach. Women came here to wash their clothes, giving rise to the name Maiden's Lane — a thoroughfare long since gone. In the 1830s it was a favourite spot for fishing and gathering mud-eels. It was turned into a quarry from the 1850s as Pyrmont sandstone became the valuable yellow building blocks for St Mary's Cathedral, Sydney University and other Victorian structures.

(10) **Sega World, One World of Sport and the Rainforest Cafe are next. Continue walking around to your right along the circular path that leads you to IMAX**, the huge eye-shaped cinema that you'll soon come to on your right. IMAX is 33 metres of screen that aims to give the viewer the ultimate out-of-body experience. The rolling-loop projection system was invented by a Brisbane man named Ron Jones. His idea was ultimately sold on to a Canadian based group who refined the technology into IMAX.

(11) **From here you can see** the suspension bridge 'mast and cable' architecture of the Exhibition Centre on the other side of Tumbalong Park. Next door is the Convention Centre which, when in full swing, seats 3500 people or divides up into 13 meeting halls — it's the biggest in Australia and in the 2000 Olympics will hold the boxing, judo, table tennis, Tae Kwon Do, weightlifting and basketball competitions.

The Aborigines called the bay Tumbalong — which means 'a place where seafood is found'. The white people first called it Long Cove because of its unusual length, then it became Cockle Bay because of its abundance of shellfish. Then in 1825 British Governor Ralph Darling arrived and decided to call the bay after himself.

(12) **Keep walking to the fore-shore of Darling Harbour's Cockle Bay.** This whole park precinct started as a 1984 state government rejuvenation scheme that took 4 years to build. Because it had always been a port for commercial shipping, the wharves and cargo holds of Cockle Bay were off limits to visitors for 150 years. The architects of modern Darling Harbour purposefully kept the new buildings low, in symmetry with the massive masonry woolstores that still lie behind it.

(13) **Face the harbour and turn left for some serious shopping in the Harbourside Shopping Centre,** the first privately funded and owned development in Darling Harbour. It's based on similar 'shopping experiences' in Baltimore and Boston. There are more than 200 shops and food outlets inside.

(14) **The Australian National Maritime Museum is just beyond.** This Museum records the history of Australia's close relationship with the sea. It's the only project in Darling Harbour funded by the Commonwealth and is the only National Museum outside the capital, Canberra. Keep an eye out for the antique vessels moored along its jetty.

The Sydney Casino is a fair walk past this point — refer to your map for access. Some walkers may prefer to catch the monorail back to the city from the Harbourside station, with a stop at the Haymarket station to visit the Powerhouse Museum.

(15) **To continue the short walk back to the city, cross the 1902 Pyrmont Bridge, now only used by pedestrians.** This swing span (which means it swings open to let boats through) bridge was hailed as a remarkable achievement in engineering. It was built at the same time as London's Tower Bridge, though completed much faster. You can easily make out the part of the bridge that swings open. This

bridge was the first in the world to be powered by electricity.

(16) **The Sydney Aquarium is underneath the bridge, take the steps down** to see sharks, crocodiles and a myriad of exotic fish lurking in huge glass tanks, or head directly back to the city. The aquarium tanks are submerged into the harbour to give the effect of walking under the sea.

(17) **Continue up Market Street to the Queen Victoria Building and underground access to Town Hall Railway Station.**

WALK 7

BALMAIN TO YURULBIN (LONG NOSE) POINT

START POINT:	Darling Street wharf, Balmain.
FINISH:	Yurulbin Point ferry.
HOW TO GET THERE:	By ferry from Circular Quay to Darling Street wharf, or by the 442 bus from the Queen Victoria Building in the city.
LENGTH:	5 kilometres.
WALKING TIME:	1 hour.
ACTUAL TIME:	2 to 3 hours.
RATING:	An easy walk with one stair climb, which can be avoided.
WEATHER CHECK:	Suitable for any weather.
REFRESHMENTS:	There's plenty of everything, particularly pubs, but very few toilets — check the map.

Suitable for strollers but not wheelchairs.

*t*his picturesque, charming walk goes through an area steeped in history. Balmain was once a working-class suburb that has now become a trendy sought-after address. Rows of pretty terrace houses, squeezed onto pocket handkerchief-sized pieces of land, line the narrow streets. The charm of yesteryear remains, and many of the earliest sandstone houses have been freshly restored. There's a pub on almost every corner, little specialty shops, and wrought-iron lace on most balconies. Tiny wooden workers' cottages dot the suburb in haphazard disarray — there are more weatherboard houses in Balmain than anywhere else in Sydney. And at the bottom of every street there's a glimpse of Sydney Harbour. Balmain was named after William Balmain, one of the surgeons on the First Fleet. He saved Governor Phillip's life by removing an Aboriginal spear from his shoulder at Spring Cove, Manly. Balmain was granted 222 hectares of land here, but sold the entire parcel for just 5 shillings to John Gilchrist, probably to repay a debt. (Like others of influence, Balmain was a liberal dealer in the rum trade.) Very little happened for the next 35 years because of the legality of the land transfer and the suburb's isolation. Cows grazed along the dirt track later called Darling Street, and the local Aboriginal Wangal clan continued fishing and gathering seafood. In the 1830s Balmain sprang to life as a maritime suburb, giving birth to a jumble of shipbuilding industries. Thomas Mort built a massive dry dock, providing employment and sparking a building boom. Many different industries were established, including sawmills, soap factories, candle manufacturers, coalmining and even a bird seed company.

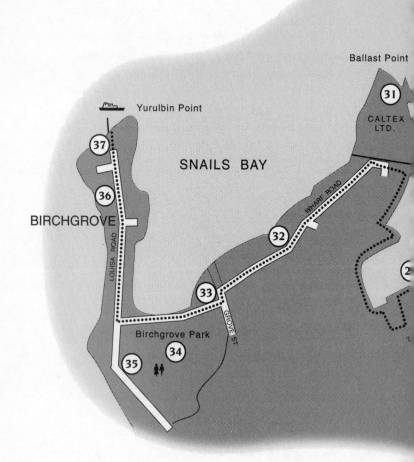

Yurulbin Point

SNAILS BAY

Ballast Point

31

CALTEX LTD.

37

36

BIRCHGROVE

LOUISA ROAD

WHARF ROAD

32

33

GROVE ST

Birchgrove Park

34

35

2

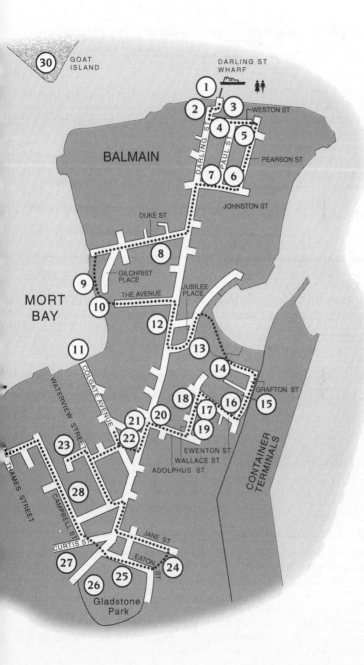

POINTS OF INTEREST ALONG THE WAY

(1) **Leave the ferry at the Darling Street wharf and look immediately to your left** to the old stone buildings where John and Thomas Fenwick began their tug service almost 130 years ago. Balmain Council plans to buy the buildings, keep the 1840 sandstone one and demolish the rest to turn the land into parkland.

(2) **On your right is Thornton Park,** part of the original land grant. It changed hands many times before being bought for parkland by Balmain Council.

One of the landowners of Thornton Park was Peter Nichol Russell, a Scot who made goldmining tools and the ironwork for Victoria Barracks in Paddington. He was so successful he donated 59,000 pounds to Sydney University to set up the Peter Nichol Russell School of Engineering. Family wealth also allowed his nephew, Impressionist painter John Peter Russell, to travel overseas to paint with Monet, van Gogh and Rodin.

(3) **On your left was the Shipwright's Arms Hotel,** known as the Dolphin Hotel in 1844, a favourite meeting place for sailors, whalers and ferrymen. Being the first port of call, young men used to 'sleep off' a heavy night in the city in the pub's cellar. It closed its doors in 1966.

Drinking was an important social pastime of early colonial life. In its heyday in the 1880s there were 43 pubs on the Balmain peninsular, which at that time took in Rozelle. Today just 22 remain.

(4) **Waterman's Cottage is next door.** Oarsman Henry McKenzie rowed patrons between Balmain and Millers Point under the Harbour Bridge. When the regular ferry service began, McKenzie was kept on, providing an after-hours service. He was still living in the house in 1907, when he was thought to be 95.

When John Gilchrist owned Balmain, he made the road that ran from one end of his property to the other and called it Darling Street after Sir Ralph, governor of the day. Darling Street was so steep the trams had to use a counterweight or dummy to prevent them from hurtling into the harbour and to help them up the incline.

Turn left up Weston Street. On the left is quiet, grassy Illoura Reserve, once a bustling shipbuilding yard.

(5) **Turn right up the steps into Pearson Street**, named after Captain Pearson. No. 11, his

house, was built in 1844. It was later renamed Eastcliffe by Theodore Jaques, who lived here until almost the turn of the century.

(6) **On the corner of Pearson and Johnston streets is No. 12 Johnston Street**, a magnificent, recently restored two-storey house. It was originally a single-storey bungalow, built by Captain Francis Hixson, Commander of the New South Wales Naval Forces. The second storey was added by Captain John Lyons in the 1860s, and he named the house Branksea. It was later to be renamed Onkaparinga, after the town in South Australia, by William Robert Snow, who ran it as a boarding house.

(7) **Just round the corner in Darling Street is No. 50**, once the Marquis of Waterford, sometimes called the Waterford Arms, and built by Sydney publican Charles Bullivant in 1846. In the 1920s the pub's 'spirits' must have inspired resident artist George Turner, who painted the ceiling. The flora and fauna masterpiece was so life-like Turner's son felt he should pick up the feathers each morning.

(8) **Walk down Duke Street to see No. 2 Duke Place**, built by Captain Robert Duke around 1840. Further down, at No. 33, is Clarenook which took ten years to build, starting in 1844. This pretty little cottage is sometimes mistaken for a house called Blantyne which stood next door, but has since been demolished.

(9) **Continue down Duke Street to the waterfront**, the home of ferries for over a century. The original Balmain company was taken over by Sydney Ferries. They moored their fleet here in Mort Bay after their Milsons Point anchorage made way for the builders of the Sydney Harbour Bridge. The State Transit

Authority is now the owner. This is also the home of Waratah Towage, which operate five harbour tugs from here and three at Port Botany. They are owned by the Adelaide Steamship company and Howard Smiths, as are Stannard Brothers, the other long-time Balmain tug operators. Their smaller tugs operate from Wharf Street in Birchgrove.

(10) Walk along in front of the houses. No. 12 Gilchrist Place is the site where Balmain Council held its first meeting in Captain Thomas Stephenson Rowntree's loft in 1860. With Rowntree's shipbuilding knowledge and Thomas Sutcliffe Mort's money, the two built Balmain's famous dry dock, sparking the industrialisation of the harbour-side suburb. Rowntree's wharf and workshop would have been just below his house.

(11) The distinctive smell of boiling tallow has now gone from the stony grey Colgate-Palmolive building at the end of the bay as production has ceased. But in its heyday the company employed hundreds making soap, toothpaste, talc and make-up. It was called 'working down the Olive' — you didn't work at Colgate, it was Palmolive. Lever Brothers, over the hill at White Bay, made Sunlight soap.

Leave the park by the first ship's propeller and turn left up the steps into The Avenue, then right into Darling Street.

Sailing and racing are synonymous with harbour life and Balmain too has played its part, holding its first regatta in 1849. The suburb has also been credited with building the first 18 and 16-footers. The 18-footers were known as 'troop carriers', as up to 15 men were needed to counterbalance the enormous sails. The Britannia, probably the most famous 18-footer, was built by Balmain local Wee Georgie Robinson in 1919. She flew 279 square metres of sail and carried a crew of 14, most of them in black and gold Balmain football jumpers.

(12) No. 117 Darling Street was the family home of Neville Wran, former premier of New South Wales (1976-86).

The Wrans' presence in Balmain goes back four generations — Neville's great-grandfather was a stonemason, working on many of Sydney's landmarks including the GPO. Neville Wran stood aside as premier in 1983 when accused at a Royal Commission of putting pressure on Chief Stipendiary Magistrate Murray Farquhar to influence the course of justice in a case involving another Balmain boy, Rugby League chief Kevin Humphreys. Wran was exonerated, but in admitting some mud would stick he made his famous remark: 'Balmain boys don't cry. We're too common and vulgar for that and probably vote Labor anyway.' Incidentally, Farquhar was later found to have influenced the case.

(13) Cross over Darling Street and into Jubilee Place and on the curve on the right-hand side is a plaque showing where the famous winged keel of Australia II, the 1983 America's Cup winner, was made. Philip Holmes, a fourth-generation Balmain sailor, and naval architect John King built the original full-sized model in secret here, and from that the mighty keel was cast.

(14) Walk over the park to Ewenton, at the end of Grafton Street, a big two-storey mansion with stunning views overlooking Cameron Cove and Johnstons Bay, named after George Johnston, Captain of Marines in the First Fleet. Ewenton was bought from builder Robert Blake by Mayor Ewen Wallace Cameron, a partner of Mort's, who added the second storey and another wing.

(15) Round the corner and fronting onto Grafton Lane is Hampton Villa (No. 12b), a charming residence built in 1855, where the 'Father of Federation' Sir Henry Parkes lived while premier of New South Wales in 1888-92. On the other side of Grafton Street is the White Bay Container Terminal, berth to huge international vessels. Originally it was the home of the 'sixty milers', the colliers bringing coal from Newcastle.

(16) Shannon Grove was built in 1848 by Balmain's first

builder, Robert Blake, who was responsible for much of the development on the point.

(17) Kinwarra, at No. 3 Ewenton Street, is prettily draped in wisteria and contains a rare sight in Balmain, a tennis court. Kinwarra is another surviving Robert Blake house. He bought just over 3 hectares of land on the point and built a total of nine houses.

(18) No. 1 Wallace Street, known as the 'Railway Station' because that's what it looks like, was built on part of Robert Blake's estate.

(19) No. 4 Wallace Street, Clontarf Cottage, was built in 1844 and is also a Blake building. It was saved from demolition by local residents and restoration began in 1988.

(20) On the corner of Adolphus and Darling streets is the Balmain Bowling Club, the site of some hot action on a Saturday afternoon. Established in 1880, it's the only club in Sydney still playing on its original ground.

(21) No. 177 Darling Street, a cute little stone cottage, was apparently built in 1843 for a barrel of rum.

(22) Next door is No. 179, the Watch House, built in 1854 to Colonial Architect Edmund Blacket's plan as a police station and lockup. The cops in those

> *Balmain also had its own colliery, part of the Bulli seam, which ran under the harbour between Mort Bay, Goat Island, Balls Head and Cremorne. Cremorne residents out-voted a commercial operation there. In 1897 'Birthday' and Jubilee' were sunk more than 94 metres below the surface at Birchgrove. It was so hot the men worked naked. Five men lost their lives when their lowering bucket caught the edge of the shaft and dropped them more than 160 metres to their deaths. The mines were shut during the Depression, but reopened to extract methane gas. The uneconomic operation was eventually closed forever in 1945, killing three more men in the shutdown.*

days were more protective than detective, hence the name 'watch' house. They locked up petty offenders, drunks and larrikins for a short time. The serious criminals went off to Darlinghurst Gaol for a much less pleasant stay. In 1920 local policeman Ira Gray, his wife and 12 of their 14 children lived there — it must have been a bit of a squeeze. Now the Watch House is the home of the Balmain Association and an art exhibition venue, open on Saturday afternoons only, between 12 noon and 3 pm.

(23) Turn down Colgate Street — you can see the other side of the factory from here. Follow the map to Balmoral House, No. 46 Waterview Street, which is actually up the lane. This gracious Georgian

sandstone residence was built by Balmain's first doctor, Frederick Harpur, in 1855. Its sweeping lawns and pretty gardens had unimpeded views down to Waterview Bay.

Retrace your steps up Waterview Street to Darling Street and over the road where there is bound to be a drinker or two leaning on the wrought-iron balcony of the London Hotel and sipping a beer. The pub has an extraordinary number of different Aussie ales, if you feel like a thirst quencher.

24 Walk up Jane Street and through the churchyards of the two St Augustine's churches. The old mossy one, now a play centre, opened in 1851. An argumentative Irishman, Father John Therry, was one of its best-known priests. It's believed he paid for St Mary's Cathedral to be built by selling some of his Pittwater land. St Augustine's was his last church — he died here in 1864. The new St Augustine's opened in 1907, and next door again is the Father

John Therry School — the lower part being the site of the first Pigeon Ground School.

25 Balmain Public School was established in 1861, and was first known as the Pigeon Ground School because it was located on Gladstone Park where pigeon shooting took place in the 1850s. Enrolments more than doubled in ten years, and a new school was built on today's site and opened in 1876.

26 Gladstone Park, formerly called Darling Park, was dug up in 1915 and a reservoir was built underneath. Following a public outcry the locals got their park back in 1918, complete with bandstand and permanent water. Today the reservoir is empty, but there are those who think it could be used to solve Balmain's parking problems — it's been proposed the 11,000 kilolitre tank could provide parking for up to 160 cars.

27 Across the road is St Andrew's Congregational

Church, built in 1855, which is where the Balmain markets are held every Saturday. Along with the usual array of stalls there's an international smorgasbord of food in the church hall.

(28) The Campbell Street Presbyterian Church was designed by Balmain mayor James McDonald and opened in 1868. The Presbyterians had a slightly chequered career in Balmain. They used to worship with the Congregationalists, but walked out after a row. They then prayed in a tent on the corner of Darling Street and Colgate Avenue before squeezing a wooden and stone church onto the strangely shaped site.

(29) Follow the map down to Mort Bay, and walk around to the dry dock site. Thomas Sutcliffe Mort had a flair for making money, firstly from wool and livestock auctions and then from land speculation. The idea of a dry dock was born, and with Captain Rowntree and merchant J.S. Mitchell as partners he formed the Waterview Bay Dry Dock company. Mort promised construction workers parcels of land when the dock was finished, and so in 1855 they

The trade union movement was already strong in the 1880s and the push was on to form a political party to look after the interests of wage earners. In 1891 the Australian Labor Party was formed at Mort Bay.

were given parts of Waterview Bay. The elite left. Mort then diversified: he made the first local locomotive, went into fresh food, cheese, coal and copper and tried his hand at exporting refrigerated meat. He succeeded second time round. Container shipping caused the death of the dock.

(30) Goat Island, out directly in front of you, was called *Mel Mel* by the Aborigines, meaning eye.

(31) Ballast Point juts out on the north side of Mort Bay, so called because the extremely heavy rock excavated there was used as ballast to steady ships.

Walk around the foreshore and when you can't go any further, climb the wooden stairs at the Yeend Street wharf to Ronald Street.

(32) The houses at Nos. 33 and 35 Wharf Road are enchanting because of their privacy. They were once an early 'semi' — one being the home of Captain William S. Deloitte and his family of seven sons. Deloitte also lived at Birchgrove House for a while. Simla and Oneida Cottage were built of sandstone in the late 1840s and have a commanding view of Snails Bay.

(33) At No. 22 Grove Street stands Whitfield, named after George Whitfield, a private of the New South Wales Corps, who was granted 12 hectares of

> *Bony Anderson, a recalcitrant convict, kept Balmain residents awake at night with his screaming from his stone bed on Goat Island. Fellow convicts etched 'Anderson's couch' out of stone for 'Wailing Charlie', who was kept on a length of chain and had his food poked to him on a stick. His chain chaffed so badly he screamed night and day. Balmain residents petitioned Governor Bourke and had him moved out of earshot. He apparently recuperated well on Norfolk Island and after a couple years without chains was single-handedly running a signal station.*

farmland around Snails Bay to Long Nose Point in 1796. Whitfield's farm was sold twice before being acquired by John Birch in 1810, and since then the district has been known as Birchgrove.

(34) Enter Birchgrove Park beside No. 22, and to your

> *The groundsman at the time, John Stephen Herrick, known as Herrick-the-Young, had to have a softly softly touch when it came to rolling the turf courts. He bound his horses' hoofs with pillows, so they wouldn't leave indentations in the grass surface. The oval also holds the record for the biggest crowd at a local cricket match. The spectators even climbed the trees to get a glimpse of Australia's most famous batsman Don Bradman play for St George against Balmain.*

left is a pretty cricket oval complete with picket fence and shady Moreton Bay figs. It was once part of Snails Bay's smelly tidal mudflats, but the land was reclaimed and filled, tennis courts and a grandstand built, and a seawall erected. The wooden platforms sticking out of the water are 'dolphins', where the New Zealand timber ships used to dock when the bay was a-buzz with sawmills.

(35) The block of home units behind the oval at No. 67 Louisa Road is the site of Birchgrove House, the first house on the peninsula, built in 1810 by John Birch.

> *Birchgrove House made it into the headlines in 1822 when Thomas Barry, a ticket-of-leave man, viciously murdered and dismembered the tenants in order to steal a silver thimble. In 1854 Hunters Hill speculator Didier Numa Joubert bought Birchgrove and subdivided it, naming Louisa and Numa streets after his family. Locals lost the battle to save Birchgrove House, and when demolished in 1967 it was the third oldest house in Sydney.*

Walk along Louisa Road, an exclusive, million dollar address, and gaze at the beautiful restorations.

(36) Raywell, at No. 144, is an attractive Georgian-style house built in 1883 with views west to Cockatoo Island.

(37) At the end of the point, at No. 150, is a Queen Anne Federation-style house more famous for its former inhabitants than its architecture. Members of the Bandido bikie gang lived here, their Harley Davidsons throbbing up and down quiet Louisa Road and their 24-hour parties keeping the locals awake. The gang came to fame after the Milperra massacre in the mid-1980s, when they and their former friends the Comancheros shot it out in the car park of the Viking Tavern, leaving seven dead. At least 40 men were imprisoned over the incident. The Bandidos were evicted from Yurulbin Point and tranquillity returned.

Before you catch the ferry to Circular Quay, walk out onto the point. Long Nose Point, or *Yurulbin* in Aboriginal, means 'swift running waters', which refers to the convergence of the Parramatta River and Sydney Harbour waters at the narrowest point between here and Manns Point. There are several Aboriginal middens around the point on private land, but art sites have been destroyed by development. It's believed the Aborigines took advantage of the point's tall cliffs and used them as a natural corral to drive kangaroos and other animals in to be killed later. The point has been returned to a people's park — the once bustling ferry-building yards of Morrison and Sinclair barely visible on the shoreline.

The bush-covered headland over the water is Balls Head, named after Lieutenant Henry Lidgbird Ball, commander of HMS Supply. Ball took the first convicts to Norfolk Island, and found and named Lord Howe Island after the British admiral who fought in the American War of Independence.

WALK 8

SYDNEY HARBOUR CROSSING

START POINT:	North Sydney railway station, Blue Street.
FINISH:	Cumberland Street, The Rocks.
HOW TO GET THERE:	By train from Wynyard to North Sydney station.
LENGTH:	6 kilometres.
WALKING TIME:	2 hours.
ACTUAL TIME:	3 to 4 hours.
RATING:	Paved the whole way, with unavoidable uphill steps out of McMahons Point and onto the Harbour Bridge; 200 steps up to the southern pylon and one uphill street climb before crossing the Harbour Bridge.
WEATHER CHECK:	The walk is suitable for any weather, but it is exposed and there is little shelter on the way.
REFRESHMENTS:	Plenty of pubs, restaurants, cafes and takeaway food shops.

Unsuitable for wheelchairs and strollers.

*t*his is a walk through history when the North Shore struggled to grow during early settlement with an almost impossible transport system to the hub of city life on the south side. This pleasant stroll starts with a mix of old and new, then meanders down convict-built streets and around the harbour's edge. You pass houses built around 200 years ago — some in near original condition — beautifully restored terraces and the modern-day mansions and town houses that fetch top dollar on Sydney's housing market. This now trendy area is fast becoming one of the most sought-after harbourside addresses. The walk is steeped in history. You will see where Billy Blue, a colourful Jamaican convict took advantage of the lack of transport to make his living rowing travellers across the harbour. The row boats were replaced with a bustling steam service that shuttled horses and coaches across the narrow spit. You will pass Luna Park, the Olympic pool with 'the view' that put Australian swimming on the map, and the Sydney Harbour Bridge — one of the modern wonders of the world. It was here that the local Aborigines fished and swam quite happily before the white man turned up with his deadly diseases, virtually wiping out their numbers in next to no time. On the harbour passenger liners and container vessels feel close enough to touch as they power by. The walk returns you to the city with an exhilarating bridge crossing and a climb up the southern pylon with spectacular views.

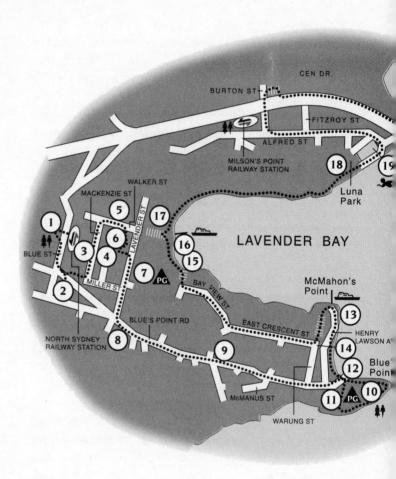

CEN DR.

BURTON ST

FITZROY ST

ALFRED ST

MILSON'S POINT
RAILWAY STATION

18

19

Luna
Park

WALKER ST

MACKENZIE ST

1

BLUE ST

5

17

LAVENDER BAY

3

6

LAVENDER ST

16

4

15

7 PG

McMahon's
Point

2

MILLER ST

BAY VIEW ST

13

8

BLUE'S POINT RD

EAST CRESCENT ST

HENRY
LAWSON A

NORTH SYDNEY
RAILWAY STATION

14

9

Blue
Poin

12

McMANUS ST

11 PG

10

WARUNG ST

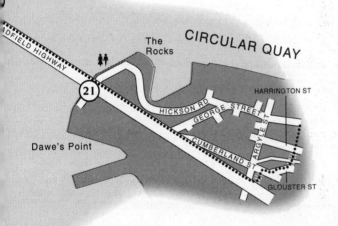

POINTS OF INTEREST ALONG THE WAY

(1) **Leave North Sydney station and walk straight across Blue Street and up the steps to the Greenwood Hotel**. This beautifully restored sandstone pub is completely dwarfed by its modern competition. The Gothic Revival structure, complete with spire, was built in 1874 as a state school. It was nicknamed Greeny's after Nimrod Greenwood, one of its headmasters. North Sydney girls' and boys' high schools, two of the North Shore's best public schools, evolved from here. The history is detailed on a plaque on the southern outside wall of the hotel. **Return to Blue Street, turn right, then take the first left into Blues Point Road.**

(2) The 27 metre spire of this pretty sandstone Presbyterian Church was used by mariners as a landmark when they sailed into Sydney Harbour in the 1860s. St Peter's is the oldest Presbyterian parish in Sydney. Various governors-general, living at nearby Admiralty House at Kirribilli, worshipped here. This was also the church of famous Australian aviator Dr John Flynn, who founded the Flying Doctor Service. His name is on pew 14. **Go down the steps from Blues Point Road, through little St Peter's Park, and turn left into McKenzie Street.**

(3) St Francis Xavier's Church and school was designed by William Wardell, architect of St Mary's Cathedral, in 1879. When the new church was turned into a war memorial in 1964, the whole northern wall was replaced with hundreds of pieces of French glass depicting the story of Christian life. The 92.6 square metre wall is believed to be the world's biggest. Carved stations of the Cross, hidden by years of paint, were also uncovered during the restoration and they're still there to see. The church is usually open.

When the white settlers first arrived the lower North Shore was inhabited by two Aboriginal tribes: the Dharug-speaking Wallumedegal clan, and the Kuringgai tribe had one clan down here, the Cammeraigals. The Cammeraigals were very powerful, and were feared and respected by other clans. They demanded a front tooth be extracted from all other natives living on Sydney's coast, and from other clans within their control. The suburb of Cammeray is now named after them, but it's thought they frequented Sydney foreshores to support their staple diet of fish and seafood. The Wallumedegal clan call their territory Wallumeda or Wallumatta, meaning opposite shore, but it later lost its Aboriginal name and became Milsons Point.

④ Across the road is St Francis Xavier's presbytery, an attractive old stone house with ornate bargeboards and ironwork. The land was originally owned by the first premier of New South Wales, Stuart Donaldson, and later sold to Mrs Collin MacKenzie. The street is now named after her.

⑤ The Royal Art Society in Walker Street is worth a visit, and glance up at the Victorian terraces Keingal, Merryula, Brenda and Glenlewis — painted in heritage colours and dating from 1880.

⑥ When the graceful Christ Church was built in 1872 the Harbour Bridge was still just a talking point. The bridegroom and guests attending the first wedding here travelled across the harbour in their carriages on the steamer *Transit*, then drove up to the church. When the bridge was finally built, however, Christ Church's minister at that time, the Reverend Frank Cash, proved to be quite a photographer, taking advantage of his magnificent harbour view from the old stone rectory next door to record the bridge's construction. **Walk down the rectory steps and cross Lavender Street.**

⑦ Look down into Watt Park, which was once a beautiful English garden. Some of the trees and palms remain. During the drought of the 1840s water from the natural stream there was collected in barrels, rowed across to Sydney and sold for 5 shillings

each. Notice the beautifully restored houses at 19 and 21 Lavender Street. No. 21 was once the coaching station for Harnett's horse buses, which ran to Chatswood and Mosman. Free rides were offered as a goodwill gesture to any stragglers found on the way.

8 Directly across Blues Point Road is the Old Commodore Hotel, originally built in 1848 by one of Billy Blue's six children, and named such after Billy. George Lavender, married to another of Billy Blue's children, was manager here when he shot himself in 1851.

9 **Wander down Blues Point Road** and soak in the atmosphere of the village: the street cafes and restored Federation-style terraces and cottages. Directly opposite the Blues Point hotel is No. 89, an original stone house with wooden shutters that looks like an old inn. Several houses still have water tanks in their gardens, and No. 74 still has steps blocking the footpath. Billy Blue's house was situated approximately on the corner of McManus Street and Blues Point Road. No. 45, recently renovated, carries the plaque 'Blue's cottage'. Maybe that was his.

10 Blues Point was named after Billy Blue, one of early Australia's most colourful convict characters. His crime was stealing a bag of sugar. In 1807, Billy became Sydney's first ferryman, rowing commuters across the

(11) **Walk up the road to Blues Point Tower**, the block of home units designed by architect Harry Seidler taking pride of place at Blues Point. This building has been given the thumbs down by Sydneysiders — it's the one they would most like to see pulled down. Walk up to the left of the building, and go down the steps to the western foreshore. Look right to Saw Millers Reserve where John W. Eaton ran a huge business, milling timbers from many parts of the world. To the left is Goat Island — called *Mel Mel* by the Aborigines, meaning 'eye' — and beyond that is the thread-like spans of the Glebe Island Bridge, irreverently dubbed 'Madonna's bra'.

(12) **Walk round the point to the eastern side** where the ferry the *Princess* made the first steam crossing in 1842. A Royal Commission in the 1890s showed five million people crossed the harbour each year; 43,800 horses and riders and 378,500 vehicles. In 1928 ferries carried a phenomenal 46 million passengers across the harbour, but by then the bridge was under construction.

(13) **Continue walking around the waterfront to McMahons Point,** named after Michael McMahon, an Irish brush and comb manufacturer who lived here. One of Australia's most famous poets, Henry Lawson walked home from the ferry down the avenue now bearing his name. The penthouse in

harbour with their horses swimming alongside. In time, Blue and his son William operated 11 boats between Blues Point, previously called Murdering Point due to its forbidding cliffs, and Millers Point on the south side.

> *Governor Macquarie nicknamed the old seadog 'Commodore of the Fleet' and gave him some land, allegedly as a bribe to watch for moonshiners. However, Billy himself was caught red-handed with two barrels of spirits lashed to his boat, and was gaoled for a year. Billy became an outrageous eccentric, dressing in an outlandish naval uniform, insisting women curtsy and men salute him. He went so far as to insist his passengers do their own rowing when he was in command.*

the La Corniche development on the point was sold for $5.1 million in 1996 — an Australian record for a home unit. The bottom floor apartment fetched $4 million the same year, breaking the previous record of $3.85 million for a Point Piper unit. **Walk behind the ferry wharf and restaurant and turn left up the public steps.**

(14) **At the top turn left down to the lookout beside the garden of No. 9 Warung Street — the view is spectacular. Return to East Crescent Street and continue along into Bayview Street**, noting the residential rebuilding on the way. **At the end go down the steps to the water.**

(15) **You're now in Lavender Bay**, also known as Quiberee Bay — the Aboriginal word for fresh water. Quiberee Bay was also known as Hulk Bay, where convicts were held waiting to be shipped to Norfolk Island or Port Macquarie. The most famous hulk, the *Phoenix*, was the only vessel to run aground on the Sow and Pigs, the submerged reef in Sydney Harbour, ending her sailing days here. George Lavender sailed to Sydney on the *Phoenix* and stayed on when it became a floating prison.

(16) Cavill's two-storey wooden swimming baths took pride of place in Lavender Bay for almost a century, and were the home of the amazing Cavill swimming family. Six of the 'Professor's' chil-

dren held Australian and world records, and son Dick developed the Australian crawl. The famous Australian artist Norman Lindsay also lived here in a waterfront house. **Walk under the first arch of the railway line into Watt Park, turn right and walk along the edge of the railway line until you come to a double row of steps.**

(17) In front of you is Quiberee, an imposing white three-storey house that used to belong to the late Australian artist Brett Whiteley. There is a section dedicated to his works at the Sydney Art Gallery and at another studio in Surry Hills. **Take the steps back to the water and continue around the seafront towards the Harbour Bridge.**

(18) Luna Park, with its grotesque grinning face, was a Sydney landmark for years. US servicemen flocked here in the 1940s with their Sydney girlfriends. Tragedy struck in 1979 when seven people died in the Ghost Train fire. The park closed down, and has since controversially re-opened several times, but without financial or popular support.

(19) Next door is the North Sydney Olympic Swimming Pool, the pool with one of the best views in the world. The saltwater pool is open all year round and in winter covered by a 'bubble' and kept at a pleasant 26°C. The pool boasts 86 world records, and the entrance tunnel is lined

with a pictorial history of Australia's swimming legends and early settlement.

(20) The roar above you is the traffic on the Sydney Harbour Bridge, which a staggering 50 million vehicles cross each year. John Job Crew Bradfield was given the task of building the bridge at an estimated cost of over 4 million pounds — it ended up costing $20 million. The granite pylons are there only for aesthetic value and have no structural purpose.

Just before the Jeffrey Street wharf in Bradfield Park is the fresh air intake for the Sydney Harbour tunnel. The exhaust fumes are piped up inside the northern pylons and let out at the top. The 2.3 kilometre tunnel was opened in 1992 and in 1997 carried 800,000 vehicles a day.

(21) **Follow the map up the hill, under the tunnel and up the steps onto the bridge. Once there stop in the middle** and imagine the two halves of 'the coat-hanger' finally coming together on a cold winter evening in 1930. Also feel the bridge sway under your feet.

(22) **At the southern pylon lookout (closest to the Opera House) climb to the top in air-conditioned bliss.** The bridge was opened in 1932. At the ceremony, Premier Jack Lang's thunder was stolen by Captain Francis De Groot, who charged past on

Not to appear dowdy beside the shiny new Glebe Island Bridge, the old coat-hanger is getting a multi-million dollar facelift in time for the 2000 Olympics. The bridge is to get a fresh coat of grey, and more staff to complete the seven-year task in three. One of the Sydney land-mark's more famous painters was Paul Hogan, whose starring role in Crocodile Dundee put the Aussie from down under on the world map.

his horse and slashed the ribbon — all because he disapproved of the premier's policies. De Groot was fined 9 pounds.

(23) **When you've finished soaking in the history and the sights, continue south across the bridge, down the steps and into Cumberland Street at The Rocks. Walk down to George Street where you can catch a bus back to Wynyard station.**

CREMORNE POINT TO MOSMAN BAY

START POINT:	Cremorne wharf.
FINISH:	Mosman Bay wharf.
HOW TO GET THERE:	By bus or train from Wynyard to Circular Quay, and then by ferry to Cremorne Point.
LENGTH:	Almost 2 kilometres — add another half kilometre for the footbridge detour.
WALKING TIME:	30 minutes.
ACTUAL TIME:	An easy hour.
RATING:	Easy: a mostly level, sealed path, with three lots of unavoidable steps — the most being a dozen.
WEATHER CHECK:	No shelter from rain apart from Cremorne Point wharf and the tree canopy.
REFRESHMENTS:	Mosman Rowers Club for drinks and meals if neatly dressed, or the cafe and general store at Mosman Bay wharf.
	Unsuitable for wheelchairs but manageable for strollers.

*t*his is a delightful, short walk around the harbour's edge. It starts at Cremorne Point, known as *Woolloorigang* to the local Aborigines, but renamed Careening Point because HMS *Sirius*, defender of the First Fleet, was refurbished upstream in Mosman Bay. The tip of the point is known as Robertsons Point after the first land owner here. Like several of the beautiful headlands around Sydney Harbour this point became a garden of fun, where revellers would cross the harbour by ferry to dance the night away. The view from the lighthouse is spectacular — you can gaze around and work out what walk you would like to do next. The path around the harbour takes you through unspoilt native bush, blending in with flats and gardens on one side and pretty gardens running down to the water on the other. You can wind your way down to the water's edge through a myriad of paths and soak in the tranquillity of bobbing boats and pinging masts. Stand in the shelter of a cave, as the Aborigines did when they came from miles around to receive their annual Christmas gift of a blanket each. The 'blackfellows', as the whites called them, were only occasional visitors to the North Shore then — around the 1860s — as their numbers had been decimated by smallpox. You emerge at the head of a narrow, steep-sided bay called *Goram-Bulla-Gong* by the Aborigines and by the earliest whites Elbow Cove because of its L shape.

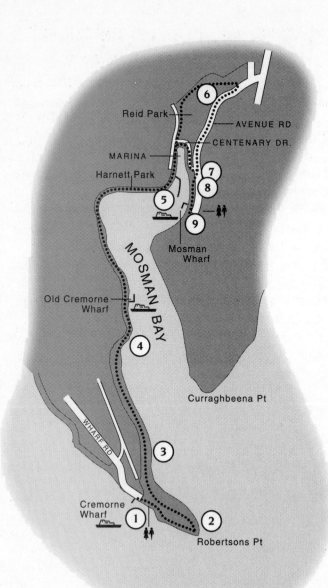

Reid Park
AVENUE RD
CENTENARY DR.
MARINA
Harnett Park
Mosman
Wharf
MOSMAN BAY
Old Cremorne
Wharf
Curraghbeena Pt
WHARF RD
Cremorne
Wharf
Robertsons Pt

POINTS OF INTEREST
ALONG THE WAY

(1) Walk up the steps beside the ferry and turn right along the sealed path into the reserve.

(2) Walk out to the point. James Robertson, a watchmaker, was granted 34.8 hectares of land here a year after he arrived on the convict transporter *Providence* in 1882, and built a magnificent house. When he sold his land, the house was turned into a hotel and the area became pleasure grounds, named after the notorious Cremorne Gardens in London. Amusements included archery, shooting, quoits, skittles, gymnastics, dancing on an enormous floor, and fireworks in the evening. Reports of boisterous behaviour of the more rowdy revellers spread and six years later Cremorne Gardens closed.

Retrace your steps past the drinking fountain, turn right and continue along the sealed path. The salmon-coloured tree with the amazing zigzag limbs is a Sydney red gum, or *Angophora costata*. It's not a true gum because of its leaf formation, but is related.

(3) After about five minutes you will come to a beautiful garden on your right voluntarily created by Lex and Ruby Graham — a plaque congratulating them can be found by the huge palm.

The difficulty of crossing the harbour was overcome in a novel manner by James Robertson's most famous son, Sir John Robertson. Rather than hire a boat to Blues Point (there was no ferry then) and walk home overland, the reckless young Robertson would swim. He undressed at Mrs Macquarie's Point, which you can see across the harbour, tied his clothes to his head and swam off. At Fort Denison he would rest before swimming the remaining distance home to Robertsons Point. Sir John went on to become New South Wales premier five times, and his statue now stands in the Domain.

Wander down through the maze of trails, which extend over the bridge down to the waterfront. In spring the orange, pink and magenta bougainvillea adds a brilliant touch of colour.

(4) When you reach the gazebo at the bottom of a pretty, sloping garden keep to the

Around 1875 a white cask was moored just off Cremorne Point and used for target practice from Mrs Macquarie's Chair. Balls from the 68 pound cannon would skim across the harbour ending up near Whiting Beach, across from you just to the left of the zoo. The barrage would stop for the hourly steam ferry, but other craft had to run the gauntlet.

middle path — the right-hand one goes down to the Sydney Amateur Sailing Club on the water. Go up three steps and continue right to the ferry pontoon. Rejoin the path and continue straight at the Bromley Avenue sign where you now have houses above and below you. When the path splits three ways at a thicket of trees, turn right down eight steps beside

Believe it or not, Cremorne Point had a chance to set up its own industry. Its very own coal seam ran about 950 metres under the sea right past the point to Balmain. In the 1890s the Sydney Harbour Mining Company was formed and exploratory bores sunk at Cremorne. Public outcry outvoted the venture, however, and the very expensive operation began at Birchgrove, in 1897.

the last house, cross a bridge and stay on the track — don't go up the steep steps on your left.

5 A little further on you will go down some steps on the right to the **3rd Mosman Sea Scouts** with Harnett Park on the left, named after Richard Harnett Snr, who was responsible for Mosman's early development. The next building is the Mosman Rowing Club, where you are welcome to drop in for a drink if you're not in your singlet and thongs, and live further than 5 kilometres away. Sydney actor John Melion, probably most famous for his role as Mick's mate in *Crocodile Dundee*, had his name stamped on a corner of the bar. He was a living advertisement for VB; and even after he passed on his voice could still be heard on the commercial.

Walk through the car park, and you can either cross the bridge and turn right to the monument dedicated to HMS *Sirius*, or keep going straight ahead on the flat grass to the sealed track leading out of the park. Oswald Bloxsome, Mosman's second resident, landed here when the water actually came up to this point. Bloxsome bought 16 hectares of land for 100 pounds, and built the amazing Rangers homestead, known as the 'pride of the North Shore'. As his guest, Oswald Brierly painted a huge mural of HMS *Rattlesnake* in a storm in the banquet hall in return for Bloxsome's hospitality, but unfortunately it disintegrated when developers tried to remove the painting, wall and all, in 1914.

⑥ **Walk up the path — the very same one that led to the Rangers more than 150 years ago, and cross the footbridge to Avenue Road.**

⑦ **Turn right and meander down to water level, to the Barn on your left,** thought to be the oldest surviving building on the lower North Shore and probably the last maritime structure dating back to early colonial times. Now used by the local scouts, the Barn was one of five stone buildings built by Archibald Mosman in 1831 to service his whaling business.

⑧ **Across the road towards the water there's a rock memorial encompassing a copper sculpture of the *Sirius*.** The tiny ship, half the size of a Manly ferry, sailed 17,566 nautical miles to Cape Town via Cape Horn to bring back fresh provisions. The ship then badly needed careening. Sirius hove to in this quiet bay, just off the ferry wharf, was pulled over on her side, had her barnacles scraped off and her hull repaired. This spot was also chosen for its remoteness, so the crew wouldn't be distracted by 'wanton women'. Before you head off see if you can hear the ghost of a green Mexican parrot calling from the old Whaling Station in the bay: 'Hurry up or you'll miss the bloody ferry'.

⑨ **Either catch the ferry back to Circular Quay from Mosman wharf or continue on the Mosman Bay to Taronga Zoo walk.**

MOSMAN BAY TO TARONGA ZOO

START POINT:	Mosman Bay wharf.
FINISH:	Taronga Zoo wharf.
HOW TO GET THERE:	Ferry from Circular Quay to Mosman Bay wharf.
LENGTH:	2.5 kilometres.
WALKING TIME:	45 minutes.
ACTUAL TIME:	1.5 hours.
RATING:	The initial climb up steep stairs and streets is tough, followed by more steps down to Little Sirius Cove. The rest is easy, apart from the short track down to the artists' camp.
WEATHER CHECK:	Not a good rainy day walk as part of the zoo track becomes slippery and sloshy under foot.
REFRESHMENTS:	A cafe and a general store at Mosman Bay wharf, and Taronga Zoo wharf also has food and drink.

Unsuitable for wheelchairs and strollers.

*t*his beautiful walk leaves the solitude of Mosman Bay where the *Sirius*, the 20-gun protector of the First Fleet, was careened just off the wharf after returning with fresh provisions from Cape Town. Shut your eyes and imagine sounds of hammering, sawing and swearing echoing around the bay. The *Sirius* could have been overhauled at Sydney Cove, but out-of-the-way Mosman Bay was chosen because there were no women of 'doubtful character' here to sidetrack the workers. They encountered other problems of isolation, however, including getting lost in the bush, either through intoxication or just bad luck. And it's been suggested they could have been killed by the Aborigines, who had lost their initial peaceful approach after being provoked by convict attacks. The walk takes you through suburban Mosman, one of the more sought-after addresses in Sydney, and down to an exquisite little park nestled at the head of Little Sirius Cove. Here is an excellent example of an Aboriginal midden — you can actually see possibly thousands of years of seafood feasting layered in the dirt in front of you. From here you meander through a tract of native bush, under the zoo wall and to the Artists' Camp where painters Tom Roberts and Arthur Streeton did some of their best work. They and a group of other famous artists lived here in tents with all the 'mod cons', painting away the days in the tranquillity of the bay.

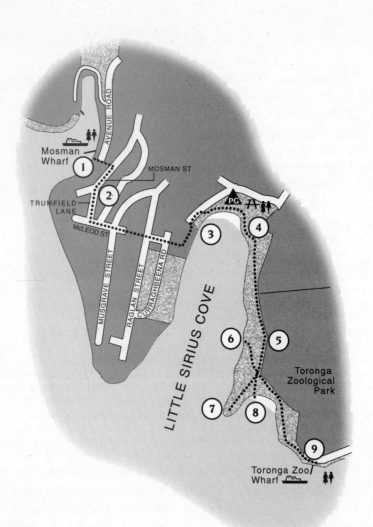

Mosman
Wharf

MOSMAN ST

TRUMFIELD
LANE

McLEOD ST

AVENUE ROAD

MUSGRAVE STREET

RAGLAN STREET

CURRAGHBEENA RD

PG

LITTLE SIRIUS COVE

Toronga
Zoological
Park

Toronga Zoo
Wharf

POINTS OF INTEREST ALONG THE WAY

(1) Go up the stairs beside the shop and cross the road directly in front of you. Stop to catch your breath.

(2) Go right up steep Mosman Road. Turn left into Trumfield Lane and left again into even steeper McLeod Street, where you can either walk up the road or the steps beside it. Cross Musgrave Street and follow the steps and pathway up beside an open car park on your left. At Raglan Street, if you are sick of steps, go right past the park and playground and turn left down Curraghbeena Road, then at the dead end turn right down the steps. Or, cross Raglan Street where it's divided, go down to the lower half of the road and keep walking down beside No. 31 McLeod Street. At the bottom of many steps turn left along a well-kept bush track below the houses.

(3) Concrete steps lead to Sirius Park. Walk round the bay and past the steps to the beach and the water bubbler, turn left beside a huge Port Jackson fig onto a sealed path.

(4) As you walk up the path notice the evidence of an Aboriginal midden — masses of shells are scattered everywhere — and across the path, where the roots of a tree are exposed, you can see in layers exactly what the Aborigines ate over possibly thousands of years. The Kuringgai-speaking Borogegal clan, numbering a few dozen, would have been responsible for this. Don't touch, and be careful where you put your feet. For this harbour-side clan, seafood and fish were their staple diet, supplemented by small animals, berries and fern roots. These Aborigines, like all others around the time of the early settlement, were not spared the ravages of smallpox, which wiped out most of their clan. The strange thing about the disease, which they called *gal-gal-la*, was that none of the whites caught it.

Turn right along the path, under the grove of melaleucas (paperbark trees), past the green Sea Scouts' den on the right. You might hear a crashing noise in the bush — it's most likely you have disturbed an eastern water dragon sunbaking. They

The last surviving member of the Cammeraigal clan was an old man called Tarpot who lived in a cave near the Barn at the head of Mosman Bay, surviving on fish and doing odd jobs. Apparently he was still alive in 1888. There's no account of when he died.

can grow up to 90 centimetres and are more frightened of you than you of them. You will pass lots of smooth-barked salmon-coloured Sydney red gums, with their wonderfully twisted branches. The Aborigines used the 'elbows' as plates. **When you come to a log across your path, walk up the 13 steps on your left and keep going. At the edge of the zoo — a concrete corner — continue under the zoo wall. Here the sealed path turns to dirt.**

⑤ A little further on you'll come to the zoo's water treatment plant, standing boldly behind wire gates for all to see. They're proud of it. Of the 400 megalitres

of water used daily, 60 per cent is recovered, cleaned and disinfected. The water is used to fill moats and toilets, water gardens and lawns and to hose down exhibits, thus saving the zoo $50,000 a year.

⑥ Just before the zoo wall takes a right-angled dog leg-left, a track on your right will take you down to the Artists' Camp. Sydney clothing manufacturer Reuben Brasch set up the camp. He used to row his family from Bondi to here and fell in love with the place. What gave the Curlew Camp distinction was the presence of two of Australia's greatest painters, Arthur Streeton and Tom Roberts, both from the

Heidelberg camp in Melbourne. They were joined by Julian Ashton, Livingstone Hopkins, Alfred Daplyn and Henry Fullwood. The camp took on an air of permanency having carpets, furniture, a wooden dining hut and even a billiards tent known as the Tabernacle. Tom Roberts' work 'Curlew Camp', an outstanding record of their bohemian lifestyle, hangs in the New South Wales Art Gallery.

At the bottom of the steps where the railing stops, the layers of rock on the corner were a permanent tent site. Go straight ahead, not towards the water, and in a rock on the right there is a plaque dedicated to Curlew Camp. Another 20 metres further along the painters left their own mark on a boulder.

⑦ **Back up top on the main path and only a metre or so further on, there's another track leading off to the right, which in three minutes will bring you out at Little Sirius Point and the harbour. Clamber down under the rock you're standing on and in the cave there's evidence of an Aboriginal midden.** You will notice that since the early settlers other people have left their mark — be careful of the broken bottles and debris.

⑧ **Retrace your steps, and 10 metres after the zoo wall takes its turn there are two half-moon stones, marking the way down to Whiting Beach.** This pretty detour will take about five minutes each way, and if you have a swim you might find a cannon ball!

⑨ **Back on the main track, cross two bridges and follow the narrow stone steps beside the water's edge.** It was about here on three separate occasions that runaway trams crashed through safety buffers and into the harbour. Luckily no-one was killed. By now you should have arrived back at the zoo wharf, from where you can **catch the ferry back to Circular Quay**. A visit to the zoo should not be missed, but that's a whole day in itself.

Around 1875 Whiting Beach became the unwitting recipient of hundreds of cannon balls. A 68 pounder at Mrs Macquarie's Chair used a mooring off Cremorne Point for target practice. The balls would skim across the harbour before sinking at Whiting Beach. The barrage would stop only for the hourly steam ferry — other craft had to take their chance.

TARONGA ZOO WHARF TO CLIFTON GARDENS

START POINT:	Taronga Zoo wharf.
FINISH:	Taronga Zoo wharf.
HOW TO GET THERE:	By ferry from Circular Quay to Taronga Zoo wharf.
LENGTH:	6 kilometres.
WALKING TIME:	2 hours.
ACTUAL TIME:	3.5 hours.
RATING:	Sealed and dirt paths around the waterline with stone steps up to the cannon, and then some occasional big uneven rock steps. From Clifton Gardens there's a steep uphill climb through suburban streets, which level out on the way back to the zoo. The walk is in the national park, so leave your dog at home. Take water, a hat, sunscreen, swimmers and a picnic.
WEATHER CHECK:	Suitable in all conditions.
REFRESHMENTS:	Food and drink at the wharf and the historic Athol Hall cafe.

Unsuitable for wheelchairs and strollers.

*t*his beautiful, easy walk wanders around the edge of Sydney Harbour, through the bushland as seen by the first settlers, past undeveloped little beaches and beside the city's historic fortifications. Sky scrapers feel within reach yet are remote from the peace of the Sydney Harbour National Park. Bradley's Head, named after the First Lieutenant on the *Sirius*, was of great strategic importance. The early settlers feared invasion — from here they could see any vessel entering the harbour. Their fears seemed justified when the colony woke one morning in 1840 to find that two American warships had slipped through the heads in the dark. Without waiting from approval from England, Governor Gipps then started financing his own fortifications. You can stand in the first gun pit built on the water's edge, and further up the headland three original cannon still stand, their muzzles pointing menacingly out to sea. There's also evidence of the original inhabitants — the Kurringgai speaking Borogegal Aboriginal clan. Several family groups roamed these foreshores, feasting on seafood and the fruits of the land, only moving on when the food ran out. The Borogegals' first encounter with the First Fleeters was friendly — they showed them where to come ashore at Koree, later renamed Chowder Bay. Clifton Gardens, as it's now known, is a big, grassy oasis surrounded by shady trees, perfect for a picnic or a swim.

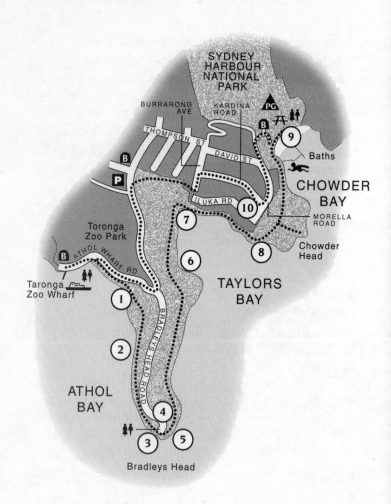

SYDNEY HARBOUR NATIONAL PARK

BURRARONG AVE

KARDINA ROAD

PG

THOMPSON ST

DAVID ST

B

Baths

P

CHOWDER BAY

ILUKA RD

10

MORELLA ROAD

Toronga Zoo Park

7

Chowder Head

8

ATHOL WHARF RD

B

6

TAYLORS BAY

Taronga Zoo Wharf

1

BRADLEYS HEAD ROAD

2

ATHOL BAY

4

3

5

Bradleys Head

POINTS OF INTEREST ALONG THE WAY

Walk up the road from the wharf and at the pedestrian crossing turn right onto the paved path. Where the road forks turn left onto the dirt track, and follow it until you come to Ashton Park.

(1) The sweeping green lawn leads to a charming, recently restored weatherboard hall, now a kiosk, dating back to the 1860s. In those days there was a pavilion, the Athol Arms Hotel, picnic grounds and a wharf to receive the visitors. But as with many of the 'fun' areas on the North Shore, the more boisterous element turned up and ruined it for everyone. There were reports of a brothel here, and women are known to have stayed away. Another furore developed: a coalmining lease was granted, but after much public protest and questions were asked in parliament, the mining was stopped. The dance hall, too, closed. In 1908, 57 hectares of this area was handed back to the people and named Ashton Park, after James Ashton, who as Minister for

The zoo put its roots down at Taronga Park in 1912, when it moved from Moore Park. Many of the animals were already accustomed to their new home as they had been quarantined around the corner.

Lands at the time pressed for the creation of the park.

Go down the steps from Ashton Park, and turn first left along the track.

(2) This stretch of water has been host to many a maritime identity. The Cunard's *Queens* anchored off here waiting to take our soldiers to the Second World War. And it was also the holding bay for the navy's mothball fleet, such as the aircraft carrier *Melbourne*, waiting to be scrapped. Back on the track, notice the magnificent Sydney red gums (*Angophora costata*) with their mottled salmon-coloured bark and their zig-zaggy branches.

(3) Around the point is Bradleys Head, known as *Burrogy* to the local Aborigines. As you come into the clearing, notice the huge Moreton Bay fig on your right, and if you look closely you can see where it was once propped up as a young tree — the stake is embedded in its trunk. On the water is a little stone wharf, where the zoo animals were landed for quarantine and which carried materials for the fortifications. The wharf is now used for wedding photos and as a viewing platform. In 1914 the German raider *Emden* was sunk with a loss of 134 lives off the Cocos Islands — HMAS *Sydney* was the victor,

and her mast stands here in memory. The circular sandstone wall to the left of the mast is a gun pit built by newly arrived convicts from Dublin. The solitary stone pillar is from the old Sydney Post Office, and measures 1 nautical mile from Fort Denison.

④ Walk around the road and go round the hairpin bend and up the convict-built steps on the high side. If you look closely halfway up, there's a defensive ditch which runs about 250 metres round the hill towards

These guns were unloaded at a North Sydney wharf and laboriously rolled through the bush to the forts. For 10 shillings a tree, locals dug out stumps blocking the route, and the path became known as Military Road. The 'Rolling of the Guns' was like a tug of war, and the toll was high. One newspaper reported: 'Such a crop of broken and twisted limbs, sprains and severe flesh wounds was seldom, if ever, known before'. It took 250 soldiers three months to roll one cannon into place.

the magnificent colours of the sandstone cave on the way down, a perfect shelter for the local Aborigines. The plentiful shellfish on the rocks would have been their staple diet, supplemented by small animals, berries, fern roots and nectar from the banksia flowers.

⑥ Return to the roadway and continue up the track to Taylors Bay, named after Lieutenant James Taylor in 1810. On a hot day you might see an eastern water dragon, and if you're really lucky you might come across a golden crown snake, which is light brown, with a golden crown on its tiny head and is about 1 metre long. They do bite, but not very hard. Unfortunately many of the reptiles in this area have disappeared as have other wildlife species, including the kangaroo and wallaby, killed off by introduced species such as foxes, dogs and cats. The area has typical Hawkesbury sandstone vegetation, with strong native under-

Military Road. This was also convict built, and you can see their trademark chips on the rocks on the high side of the trench. **Continue up the steps.** In 1871, the year of the Russian scare, this gun pit, an underground powder magazine and a stone firing gallery for riflemen were built — just in case there was a land invasion. Three 68 pound cannon and two 80 pounders all made it safely to Bradleys Head.

⑤ Retrace your steps back to the hairpin and take the steps down to the beach. Notice

In an account to England Bradley described these Aborigines as being a rusty kind of black and abominably filthy. 'They smear animal fat on their bodies and are covered in every sort of dirt. They are entirely naked and have no fixed place of residence.' The men sometimes wore nose-bones, stuck kangaroo teeth, fish jaws or feathers in their hair, and had raised scarring on their torsos.

growth that attracts many small birds like the scrub and blue wrens and red-tailed finches. If you stay still and whistle, they will come down to investigate.

(7) On the corner of Taylors Bay there's a lush pocket of rainforest nestled in a natural stream, dotted with native ferns and rock orchids. Aboriginal engravings of kangaroos can be found on a rock face. Such vertical carvings are rare in Sydney.

Taylors Bay was where one of the three midget Japanese submarines was blown up during the Second World War after entering Sydney Harbour on a raid against Allied shipping. Torpedoes narrowly missed the USS Chicago, but tragically hit HMAS Kuttabul at Garden Island, killing 21. One of the two-man subs was caught in anti-submarine netting off Middle Harbour and blown up by its crew, the other disappeared.

(8) **Round the corner you come to a block of houses above. Keep going past until you come to a 'T' junction. The right-hand track goes down to Chowder Head on a narrow path (four minutes each way). About 20 metres from this junction on the main track, take the right fork and keep going until you come to a grass clearing. Go down the steps and follow the water around to Clifton Gardens.**

(9) **Clifton Gardens** was originally called Chowder Bay by the American whalers, who made chowder from the oysters growing on the rocks. The owner of the whaler *Lady Wellington*, Captain Cliffe, bought 6 hectares of land here and built a house called Cliffeton. The Clifton Arms Hotel was built in 1871. Three storeys were later added and it was renamed the Marine Hotel. Sydney Ferries Ltd were the next owners around 1906, buying the hotel and pleasure grounds, which included a huge dance pavilion. They added a giant circular swimming pool, advertised it as the largest in the southern hemisphere with seating for 3000, and brought picnickers in by the ferry load.

Once again larrikins turned up and one witness recalls their idea of amusement was to 'put a rock in the end of a sock and go down to Chowder Bay'! They dressed like London hoods with bells tied to their boots. The women were worse than the men and when an Amazon known as Bonnie Black Bess went on the rampage, the police weren't game to go near her.

(10) **Leave the gardens on the path by the phone box, and walk up beside the tiny park, the site of the hotel.**

(11) **Follow the map and when you turn right into Kardina Street, look straight ahead to**

Early in the 1820s Governor Macquarie gave a piece of land at Georges Heights (on the right-hand hill) to King Bungaree, one of the more colourful and better known Aborigines from the Broken Bay tribe. He and 16 other families were to farm the land, but the natives ate all the seeds and returned to their nomadic life. King Bungaree was often to be seen in cast-off naval uniforms — and his wife, Queen Goosberry, who also cut a bizarre figure, would insist on being kissed when met. She apparently stank of fish oil and was described as 'a personification of ugliness'. King Bungaree became the first Aborigine to circumnavigate Australia when he accompanied Matthew Flinders and Phillip King. He loved a drink and died an alcoholic in 1830.

the Manor. Still the largest single house in Mosman, the Manor was built before the turn of the century. It was originally called Bakewell's Folly, after its builder. The Theosophical Society, which established radio 2GB in Sydney, then bought the Manor. (GB stands for Giordano Bruno, the Italian philosopher who inspired the Theosophists.)

Follow the map back to the zoo wharf, and catch the ferry back to Circular Quay.

WALK 12

THE SPIT TO MANLY

START POINT:	Spit Bridge.
FINISH:	Manly wharf.
HOW TO GET THERE:	Catch the 190 bus from Wynyard station to the western side of Spit Bridge.
LENGTH:	Almost 10 kilometres.
WALKING TIME:	3.5 hours.
ACTUAL TIME:	4 to 4.5 hours.
RATING:	This is a LONG walk and should not be tried unless you are moderately fit and have walked this distance before. The numerous steps to Crater Point lookout are the most difficult part. The walk is best done from the Spit because the uphill section is near the beginning when you're fresh. A hat, water and good shoes are essential, and take a picnic and your swimmers. Leave your dog at home as most of the walk is in the Sydney Harbour National Park.
WEATHER CHECK:	Not recommended on a rainy day or an extremely hot one.
REFRESHMENTS:	There's a kiosk and restaurant at Clontarf, though they're not always open, then nothing until the marina at Forty Baskets Beach, where you can buy a drink. At Manly there's everything.

Unsuitable for wheelchairs and strollers.

*t*he Spit Bridge to Manly walk is recognised as the most picturesque on the North Shore, and takes in some of most sensational scenery in Sydney. It encompasses spectacular views of Sydney Harbour and its entrance and contains native bush that has changed little since the arrival of the First Fleet in 1788. The walk meanders along the coast beside secluded white sandy beaches and luscious subtropical rainforest and groves of Sydney red gums. In spring the wildflowers form a mantle of colour, and in winter it's the brilliant yellow of the wattle trees that warms the day. The whole area is rich in Aboriginal history. The Kuringgai-speaking Aborigines who lived here called the spit *Burra Bra*. They frequented the sheltered waters around Fisher Bay and Clontarf, which were perfect for fishing and gathering crabs and shellfish. Further on there's an excellent Aboriginal engraving site which tells a picture story about their ancestors. Each successive Aboriginal generation would have to re-groove the engravings to keep contact with the Dreamtime. You pass the precariously perched Crater Cove huts where the original builders escaped the rush and bustle of Balmoral to eat freshwater yabbies, grow vegetables and ride the deadly bombora at their doorstep. These huts are being kept as a monument to those who lived in the various camps around the harbour in the early 20th century without having to pay millions of dollars for the real estate. Reef Beach was one of those camps, but more recently gained notoriety for nudity. After walking through this page of history, you come back to civilisation — modern harbourside suburbs with million dollar homes and marinas bursting with yachts.

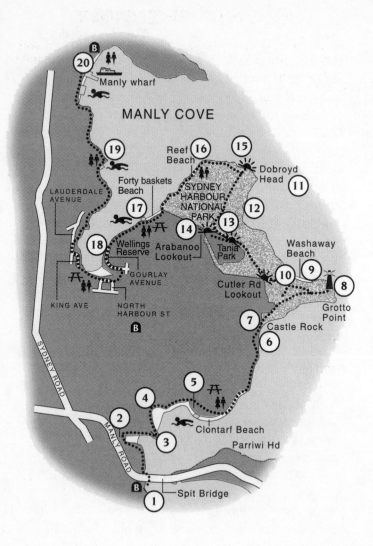

MANLY COVE

Manly wharf

Reef Beach

Dobroyd Head

SYDNEY HARBOUR NATIONAL PARK

Forty baskets Beach

LAUDERDALE AVENUE

Wellings Reserve

Arabanoo Lookout

Tania Park

Washaway Beach

GOURLAY AVENUE

Cutler Rd Lookout

Grotto Point

KING AVE

NORTH HARBOUR ST

Castle Rock

SYDNEY ROAD

MANLY ROAD

Clontarf Beach

Parriwi Hd

Spit Bridge

POINTS OF INTEREST ALONG THE WAY

(1) Get off the bus immediately after it crosses Spit Bridge and take the stairs under the bridge to the grassy area on the other side, called Ellerys Punt Reserve. At the water's edge on the right is all that's left of the old punt ramp, which must be close to the spot where local resident Peter Ellery started the first hand punt service in 1880. The government then updated to steam, linking the horse-drawn service to Manly. By 1924 passengers could leave the electric tram at The Spit, cross over a new bridge, and join another tram about where you're standing to continue the journey to Manly. The tram system closed in 1939, and the present Spit Bridge opened in 1958.

(2) Head off on what was the old tram track, and tucked away behind secluded Fisher Bay is a wet pocket of subtropical rainforest. The water gum with its strange bark lines the creek at the head of the bay. Most of the rainforest species have been named, including the lilly pilly, whose fruit was a plentiful food source to the local Aborigines.

(3) Continue around the bay and near the point is an Aboriginal midden — it's not in just one neat pile, but thousands of discarded shells litter the undergrowth. Take a seat at the lookout and catch your first glimpse of the Spit and Middle Harbour.

(4) Continue around Sandy Bay, where at low tide the receding water leaves boats lying on their sides and crabs scuttling for cover.

(5) Wander on past the marina to Clontarf reserve and beach — named *Warringa* by the local Aborigines. This was a favourite picnic site for the early settlers, with ferries bringing in as many as 6000 people on a hot summer's day. It was at a picnic here in 1868 that the Duke of Edinburgh was lucky to survive an assassin's bullet. Irishman Henry James O'Farrell fired twice at point-blank range. Prince Alfred was apparently saved by the thickness of his braces. The royal wound recovered quickly, but O'Farrell was executed for his

After the shooting incident Clontarf's party reputation spread, but it wasn't all good news. Claims of loutish and licentious behaviour hit the headlines. After a write-up of an extremely rowdy Boxing Day party the owners sued the Bulletin *— and won. But the victory was a hollow one as the judge awarding damages of just one farthing!*

crime. In the picnic shelter closest to the water there's a pictorial
account of the event.

**Keeping the water on your
right, head towards the concrete wall and walk in front of
the ugly concrete sewer tower.
Continue along the beach, past
the palm on the point and in
front of the row of houses.**
When the sewer was being built,
workers didn't bother with boats
— they just walked from one side
of Middle Harbour to the other,
inside the pipeline. **At the end of
the beach, head up the bush
track to Castle Rock Beach.**

⑥ **Just before Castle Rock you
cross a bridge then join the
concrete footpath from Ogilvy
Road. Turn right down four
small flights of stairs onto
Castle Rock Beach for a rest.**

⑦ **Go back up one flight of
steps, then turn right into
the National Park.** All flora,
fauna and Aboriginal sites are
protected here, and dogs aren't
allowed. You're now in a Sydney
red gum forest (*Angophora costata*),
which have outstanding, smooth
salmon-coloured trunks and wonderfully contorted boughs. These
handsome trees actually aren't
true gums — you can tell by the
positioning of leaves on the
mature tree. These are opposite
rather than alternate. Possums
and kookaburras often make their
homes in the hollows of dead
branches. The noisy birds overhead are brilliantly coloured rainbow lorikeets sucking nectar from
the flowers. **Follow the track up
the stone steps and along the
wire fences until you reach the
sign 'To Grotto Point Light or
Cutler Road Lookout'. Either
carry on in a northeasterly
direction or go down the ridge
to Grotto Point, where the track
gets much rougher and steeper.**

⑧ **The area around Grotto
Point and back up to the
main track is unfenced. Don't
go too close to the edge, and
supervise your children.** Grotto
Point gets its name from the

caves or grottoes where the Aborigines sheltered around the shoreline. Look out for the grass trees (*Xanthorrhoea*) with their long grass-like leaves and tall, central stem used by the Aborigines as spears. They would join three lengths with yellow glue from the base of the tree and fasten hardwood prongs, tipped with bone, with the same resin. This fruiting stem generally only flowers after a bushfire. It was at Grotto Point that a First Fleet survey party camped just two days after dropping anchor in Port Jackson. The lighthouse, built in 1911, lights

the way for ships entering the harbour when lined up with the Parriwi light at Mosman.

⑨ Make your way back up the ridge. Below you is Washaway Beach, so named because of the exposed rocks left by pounding seas washing the sand away. About 50 metres after your track rejoins the main one you will come to a seat.

⑩ Immediately on your right is a small kangaroo carved in the centre of the track, indicating an Aboriginal engraving site.

Treat the engravings with respect, and don't stand on them or touch them. A few metres seawards there's a 3 metre wide carving of a huge kangaroo with its tail buried. Walk on towards the cliff edge and on your right is an Aboriginal fish carving. About 4 metres to the left, still looking to sea, is another, and 13 metres further left again is a giant kangaroo (if you look hard) and inside is a dolphin. Retrace your steps back to the first fish. With the sea at your back, about 6 metres in front of you in reddish stone is an emu. Generally, a group of engravings such as this tells a story. The fish, animal and bird grouping here is probably telling about ancestral activities during the Dreamtime. The engravings would be made by an artist or a tribal elder, who would first make an outline with a sharp stick or ochre. He would then punch a series of holes around the outline which was sometimes left, but usually cut into a smooth continuous groove. Initiation ceremonies of young Aboriginal men were often held at engraving sites, but not at this one. There's been no recorded initiation ceremonies between Port Jackson and the Hawkesbury, except for one at Farm Cove.

Rejoin the main track. Stay quiet for a while and you may spot a Burton's legless lizard, a copper-tailed skink or an eastern water dragon sunbaking. The wattle (*Acacia*) in this area brings a welcome warmth to winter.

(11) **Off Dobroyd Head are three buoys marking the dangerous Gowlland Bombora** where Staff Commander John Gowlland and Henry Peterson drowned while surveying Middle Harbour in 1874. Their boat was swamped by a dumper breaking on the unseen reef. These were the first of about 40 people to perish on the bombora. It also claimed bodies, and all variety of pleasure craft after breaking away from their moorings.

The bombora also trapped the crew of the South Curl Curl lifeboat. They had rowed up the coast on a training run, saw a fantastic wave breaking in the harbour, caught it, lost it, and crashed onto the rocks. The lifesavers were plucked from the water by Crater Cove residents and the story emerged. The boat was new, so new it had only been delivered that day and was yet to be christened by sponsors!

(12) **Look closely at the cliff top back from Dobroyd Point and you will see the Crater Cove huts precariously perched there.** The first was built in 1923 by Bob Cadwell, George Mennis and Fritz Petersen from driftwood brought in by the southerly buster they called the 'Woodwind'. The 'Crow Tribe' was formed as crows, kitty hawks and sea eagles had become part of everyday life — the password 'kaaak' was sounded by members entering the cove. The huts are now being preserved by direct relatives of the original owners, under the watchful eye of the National Parks and Wildlife Service.

(13) **Where the track flattens out you will come to the spectacular Crater Cove lookout,** and above you is Tania Park, named after Manly beauty Tania Verstak, who was crowned Miss Australia in 1961 and Miss International the following year.

(14) **At the Manly end of the park is the Arabanoo Lookout,** named after an Aboriginal who was reluctantly captured by Governor Phillip at Manly Cove, but died within six months of smallpox, after helping his 'brothers' infected with the same disease.

Retrace your steps to Crater Cove and rejoin the track. The vegetation has changed again to stunted heath, densely clumped together because of constant exposure to the wind. She-oaks (*Casuarinas*) with their cone-like seed pods dominate the Dobroyd headland. In spring the male sports an orange flower; the female produces the nuts, and like many Australian natives, she-oaks need fire to release their seeds. This area becomes a paint-box of colour when the wildflowers blossom in spring.

(15) **The track now becomes a bit rugged and steps down towards Dobroyd Point**, famous for its kite and model plane flying at weekends. **Near the bottom you can take the left turn which is a short cut to Manly or continue straight down to the lookout.**

> *Keep you eyes peeled for a fairy penguin in the sea or even inland on the track. The tiny breeding colony has been put on the endangered species list because of the loss of habitat. In 1954, when the colony numbered around 600, half were shot in a random attack. Those caught injuring protected native fauna face two years' imprisonment or a $200,000 fine.*

(16) **The track meanders around to Reef Beach**, also known as Pirates Camp, which sprang up in 1834 as a little canvas refuge on private land with only water access. By the end of the century the tents had given way to more permanent structures, and the land had been taken over by the Crown. The local rugby football club, then called Federals, had a camp here, and like any good resort it had its own two hole golf course — with a tee and green at each end of the beach. Reef Beach's most famous claim to fame, however, is its nudity. It

first went topless in 1975, and nude shortly after. Controversy raged for years, but finally the locals won and Reef Beach lost its 'official' nude status in 1996. The Aborigines made first use of the beach, of course, taking advantage of the good shellfish supply and sheltered fishing. A midden stretches almost the whole length of the back of the beach, but just looks like a pile of shells now. If you're very lucky you may see their carvings of fish and shields on the tessellated rocks, but they're usually only visible after a storm.

Leave the beach at the other end and continue along the track in dappled light under the canopy of tall natives.

(17) **Next is Forty Baskets Beach,** named after the 40 baskets of fish sent across the water to a contingent of Sudanese troops in quarantine at North Head in 1885. This eastern-facing beach with views to Manly is particularly pleasant in the early morning and is protected by a shark-proof net.

(18) **Continue on the track, past boatsheds until you reach Gourlay Avenue.** The area of bush on your right is Wellings Reserve where Aborigines lived in rock shelters until disease brought by the white man wiped many of them out. **Near the first houses on the right follow the path across the little bridge then turn down North Harbour**

Street. Cross the park near the water's edge and at the end climb the steps to King Avenue. Wind up and around to Lauderdale Avenue, then head down the path to the right, which will lead you around the waterfront.

(19) **Fairlight Beach** is named after Fairlight House, built by Manly's great benefactor Henry Gilbert Smith in 1854. Some of the garden, three Norfolk Island pines and the stone wall are all that remain.

(20) **Continue on past Oceanworld and the Manly Art Gallery (both worth visiting on another day) and on to Manly wharf. Catch the ferry or jetcat back to Circular Quay or the 144 bus to Wynyard station.**

WALK 13

MANLY TO SHELLY BEACH TO SPRING COVE

START POINT:	Manly wharf.
FINISH:	Manly wharf.
HOW TO GET THERE:	By ferry or jetcat from Circular Quay to Manly, or a bus from Wynyard station to Manly.
LENGTH:	6 kilometres.
WALKING TIME:	1.5 hours.
ACTUAL TIME:	3 hours.
RATING:	Fairly easy: mostly paved along flat paths and undulating streets — the walk along Collins Beach is the exception.
WEATHER CHECK:	Suitable in rain or shine with appropriate clothing.
REFRESHMENTS:	Everything at Manly, a restaurant and kiosk at Shelly Beach, and a kiosk at Little Manly Cove.

Only suitable for wheelchairs and strollers from Manly wharf to Shelly Beach and back.

'Seven miles from Sydney and a thousand miles from care' was how this historic Australian beach resort was described in its halcyon days. After an exhilarating trip up Sydney Harbour you will enter the sanctuary of Manly Cove, just as Governor Arthur Phillip did in January 1788, except he rowed in. It was Phillip who named the area Manly, so impressed was he by the confidence and 'manly' appearance of the Aborigines who met him. Manly might have been the most perfect position in the new colony, but with poor access and unfertile land settlement was slow to get going. That was until English entrepreneur Henry Gilbert Smith, later known as the Father of Manly, set foot here. The walk takes you down the changing face of the Corso, a footpath to the sea for thousands of years to the Cannalgal and Kayimai people. With the seabreeze in your face, you have just walked out onto one of the most beautiful beaches in the world, with its 2 kilometres of golden sand and its landmark Norfolk Island pines. A visit to Manly isn't complete without eating fish and chips on the seawall while the seagulls fight for tidbits. Manly was seen as a cure-all for many illnesses, including the overworked livers of the high-living Victorians and for 'ennui' — boredom common among upper-class ladies! From Manly your walk passes magical little Shelly Beach, the ruggedness of the ocean cliff-face, right past that castle on the skyline — St Patrick's College — before heading back to the harbour. You walk on the very same Collins Beach where Governor Phillip was speared by an Aborigine, and on around the bays back to Manly wharf.

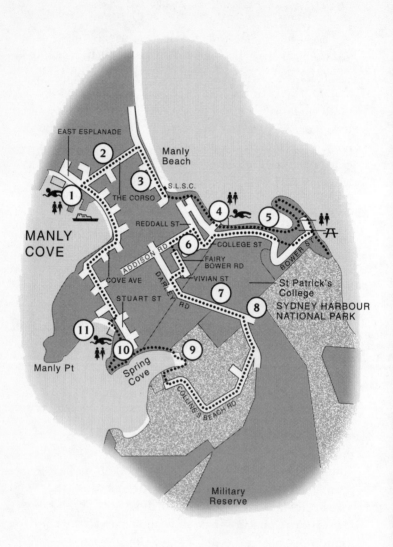

POINTS OF INTEREST ALONG THE WAY

(1) **The walk starts at Manly wharf,** built by Henry Smith in 1855. He also started the first ferry service. His paddle-steamer called the *Phantom*, sometimes also called Puffing Billy, began the first regular service, taking more than an hour to reach Sydney on a rough day. If there were sufficient theatregoers wanting to go to the city at night the *Phantom* would take them. The captain would roast potatoes in the ferry's furnace, and serve them with whisky and coffee on the way back — starting the Hot Potato Club!

> *Developing Manly as a seaside resort became Henry Smith's passion. He built the first hotel, then cleared a narrow swamp to link the harbour and the sea. He called this the Corso, after a favourite street in Rome.*

(2) **At the head of the Corso** look left through the archway of fig trees to the town hall. The mature trees gracing the centre of the Corso date back to Smith's time. The war memorial straight ahead was built in memory of Manly's first soldier to fall in the First World War — Alan David Mitchell.

St Matthew's Anglican Church was originally designed by influential 19th century architect Edmund Blackett in 1864. Sandstone from the original church was reused when the new Gothic Revival-style church was built when the Corso was widened. The stained glass windows are exquisite. There's a fascinating collection of 1870s Victorian, Georgian and Elizabethan Revival-style buildings at first floor level on the ocean side of the Commonwealth Bank. Take in the shipshape look of the New Brighton Hotel when you look back on her 'bow'. And in an even more maritime flavour are the fort-like qualities of the Steyne Hotel which guards the ocean end of the Corso.

Smith planted Manly's first legendary and now heritage-listed Norfolk Island pines. Stretching from Manly to Queenscliff, they flourished for almost a century until southeasterly winds carrying pollutants from the North Head sewerage outfall started killing them. The council has come to

> *During the Second World War Manly Beach was covered in coils of barbed wire, and the order was given to cut down the pines as the enemy could recognise Sydney by them. There was a public outcry and all the pines but one survived, which was cut down to give a gun emplacement a clear view of the beach!*

The bronzed Aussie surfing reputation got off to a rough start around the turn of the century when swimming was banned during daylight hours and men and women kept at separate ends of the beach. The local newspaper editor ran the gauntlet and walked into the surf in broad daylight, but, 'third time unlucky', he was arrested. After a yearlong campaign the rules were changed, but at a cost: all swimmers aged 18 and over had to wear neck-to-knee bathing suits.

the rescue and is replanting Manly's landmarks.

(3) Opposite the beach is the Far West Children's home where country children who have never seen the sea before are brought to Manly for medical treatment. This facility started in 1925 when 58 disabled children, suffering from the effects of heat, dust and flies, made the first pilgrimage to the sea.

Head off now past the Manly Surf Club, which could be mistaken for a deck on a P&O liner.

(4) Take in the charm of Fairy Bower, where once there was a maze, wild violets, maidenhair ferns and tracks leading in and out. Now there are seats dedicated to Manly 'legends' and a rock that fell from the cliffs above. You are actually walking on the first sewer line that ran between Manly and Cabbage Tree Point, where sewage was discharged into the ocean rather than into the already polluted harbour.

(5) Shelly Beach is free from the onshore winds and the surf and sheltered by beautiful coral trees. The restaurant is a favourite spot — romantic at night, or just relaxing by day with its peaceful outdoor ambience

The first official lifeguard, Happy Eyre, was employed by Manly Council in 1907 and he patrolled at North Steyne on alternate Sundays. Incidentally, he was a New Zealander.

and the company of little sparrows pecking from your table.

Either climb the steps on the left of the beach or walk up the path straight ahead. Where they converge, head left around the track on the cliff top. Follow the path (but dart off to look at the spectacular ocean view) until you reach the end of the car park. Looking out to sea, the most distant headland to your right is North Head. Now bring your eye back to the closest high point on the skyline, with a cave underneath. There's a track to that point through the bush (about three minutes each way) — take the right fork, which leads round the side of the rock to a seat under the shelf. New Zealand is out there somewhere.

Retrace your steps and walk up Bower Street. Take a short cut across the park in front of the two giant Moreton Bay figs, catching glimpses of the view enjoyed by residents of this desirable Manly address. **Turn left into College Street** and walk up through the grove of paperbarks.

⑥ Round the corner is the 'pebble house' called Logan Brae, a cute Californian bungalow-style house with pebble pylons, timber

facades and low-pitched gables.

⑦ **In Addison Road take the public stairway beside No. 130, which leads into Fairy Bower Road. At the intersection of Vivian Street is the best view of St Patrick's College.** This majestic building towers above Manly with uninterrupted views north to Terrigal and south to the city. The Catholic church built the seminary and Archibishop's House over the road. Sheerin and Hennessy were the architects and the seminary was opened in 1889. The International College of Tourism and Hotel Management moved in when the priests moved to Strathfield at the end of 1995.

⑧ **Continue up the road past Manly Hospital to the Parkhill Sandstone Arch,** the entry to Sydney Harbour National Park. **At the Collins Flat signpost turn right and walk to the end**

of the road through a very beautiful stretch of Australian bush. **At the gates to the Australian Police College,** formerly the Venereal Diseases Hospital, **take the bush track on your right.**

⑨ **After crossing two wooden bridges the track turns left down to Collins Beach,** still in its virgin state apart from the dead eucalypts and the washed-up rubbish. This is how the beach would have appeared to Governor Phillip and Captain Collins when they disembarked here in September 1790 to catch up with their friend Bennelong, who had been walkabout. Three men had died after a whale tipped up their punt in the harbour, and the whale was then washed up in Manly Cove and killed by the local Aborigines. News spread fast and hundreds of Aborigines from near and far turned up for a feast. Bennelong was introducing some of his friends when Governor Phillip was speared through the right shoulder, just above the collarbone. A West Head tribe Aborigine, Wil-le-me-ring, mistook his outstretched arms for a hostile gesture. Phillip recovered and the Aborigine was left to be dealt with by his peers. After the incident the beach was named after the Judge Advocate George Collins.

Leave the beach at the northern end via the rough cut steps, then follow the concrete path alongside the back wall of the Archbishop's House, which is also known as the Cardinal's Palace, until you emerge at Stuart Street.

(10) **Walk into the landscaped grounds of the old gasworks,** demolished in 1970. Meander around this well laid out site, and read about its history and see the various pieces of memorabilia. Coal was first brought here by the little colliers known as the Sixty Milers — the distance from Newcastle to Sydney by sea. In 1883 the Manly Gaslight and Coke Company was formed, and after a later name-change it was taken over by the North Shore Gas Company, producing its last gas in 1964. Look back at the serenity of Spring Cove, from where you've just come, and next door to sleepy Store Beach and then on to Quarantine Beach and the Quarantine Station where immigrants with infectious diseases

were held. The point beyond the jetty is Cannae Point, after *Canna*, the Aboriginal name for the Manly area.

(11) **Leave the old gasworks and walk around the footpath to the charming, sheltered beach and netted pool at Little Manly Cove.**

Follow the map back to Manly wharf and catch the ferry or jetcat back to Circular Quay.

WALK 14

MANLY TO NORTH HEAD TO QUARANTINE STATION

START POINT:	Manly wharf.
FINISH:	Quarantine Station or Manly wharf.
HOW TO GET THERE:	By ferry or jetcat from Circular Quay to Manly, or the 190 bus from Wynyard station to Manly wharf.
LENGTH:	10 kilometres.
WALKING TIME:	1.5 hours (walking the Quarantine Station: 1–1.5 hours).
ACTUAL TIME:	3.5 to 4 hours.
RATING:	The walk is long on roads and paths with a steep climb through suburban streets to North Head Reserve.
WEATHER CHECK:	The walk on the exposed headland is miserable in the rain and not recommended on an extremely hot day.
REFRESHMENTS:	You can get everything at Manly wharf, and the Manly Hospital shop in Darley Road is open every day for snacks.

Suitable for strollers if you like a push; unsuitable for wheelchairs.

*t*his walk is one of the most spectacular in the Manly area. North Head dominates the entrance to Sydney Harbour and thousands of sightseers visit every year just to soak in the view. Out there at the end of the northern peninsula it's mesmerising to watch the ocean rollers break hundreds of metres below, then see the swirling water get sucked back out in a white whirl of foam. North Head is much grander than its southern counterpart, and towers over the entrance to the harbour. It was known as *Boray* to the local Aborigines. Governor Phillip was so impressed with the confidence and manly behaviour of the Aborigines who first met him in 1788 that he called the area where you start your walk Manly. The fairytale palace on the skyline becomes a reality when you pass St Patrick's gates, but the tranquillity has been shattered by the tug of war between Manly Council and the Catholic church over development of the site. The walk takes you through the Quarantine Station at Spring Cove, which battled for more than 150 years to stop diseases such as small-pox, scarlet fever and the plague spreading through the fledgling colony. The station is all still there, only the inmates have gone — but their ghosts live on. Visitors can walk through the hospital where everything is still intact; feel the chill of the burial grounds where hundreds were entombed, see the extensive sterilising system which doesn't look unlike a gas chamber, and read the exquisite rock carvings etched by inmates waiting for their freedom. The Quarantine Station tour, run by the NPWS starts at 1.10 pm every day, but must be booked by phoning 9977 6522. There is a fee.

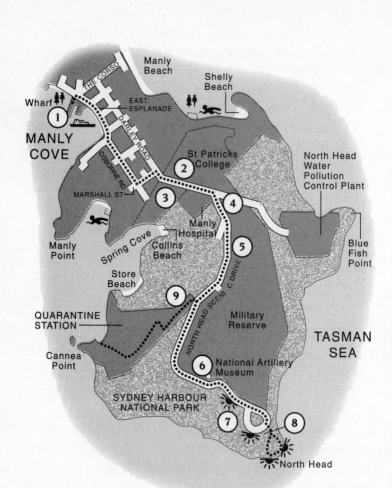

POINTS OF INTEREST ALONG THE WAY

(1) **Leave Manly wharf and follow the map until you get to St Patrick's College.**

(2) Majestic St Patrick's takes pride of place above Manly with uninterrupted views north to Terrigal and south to the city. After a protracted battle with the basically Protestant government of the day, the Catholic church finally succeeded in getting 24.3 hectares here to build the seminary and Archbishop's House over the road. Sydney architects Sheerin and Hennessy designed this building in Neo-Gothic and Romanesque style in 1885. The rustic sandstone was quarried on the headland, and the building is richly decorated inside and out with intricate carvings, statues, columns and stone verandahs. The priests moved to Strathfield at the end of 1995 and the International College of Tourism and Hotel Management moved in. Controversy erupted again over development plans. The Land and Environment Court gave approval for about half of the residential development sought by the Catholic church. Proposals for aged and child-care facilities, a nunnery and a Bear Cottage hospice for terminally ill children haven't been finalised.

(3) Over the road is the Archbishop's House (affec-tionately known as the Cardinal's Palace) which was built by the same architects, but slightly before the seminary. It is an outstanding example of Gothic Revival architecture. The Archbishop hasn't actually lived here for around 40 years — seminary staff did when the priests lived over the road. The seminary and the house were dissected by North Head Road in 1914.

(4) **Continue up the road past Manly Hospital to the Parkhill Sandstone Arch, the entry to Sydney Harbour National Park.** This area was opened in 1927 so the public could stand on North Head and greet the Duke and Duchess of York as they sailed into Sydney. If you look left before you go through the arch, notice the high sandstone wall dogleg, then head off towards the coast. This wall was built after the locals complained the Quarantine Station was monopolising 307 hectares of land at the entrance to the world's most beautiful harbour. The federal government leased 121 hectares to Manly Council for 1 pound a year on the condition it build the 3 metre high sandstone wall. The council couldn't afford the 18,000 pounds for the constructions, but Archdale Parkhill, former Manly councillor and then federal government cabinet minister, came to the rescue

with a federal grant. The Parkhill Reserve was officially opened in 1933.

(5) This wasn't the end of the land grab, however, as the School of Artillery on the left-hand side was to have its section carved off too.

(6) **Keep walking past the Quarantine Station on your right and the next point of interest is the Artillery Museum and North Fort on your left, well worth a visit another time.** Visitors can walk through the tunnel fortifications and see the huge gun emplacements, where a battery of 9.2 inch guns could send a shell 28 kilometres out to sea. The museum is also well worth a look with an interesting range of defence equipment dating back to the 1800s.

(7) **Stop at the next lookout on your right to soak in the view.**

(8) **The Fairfax Walking Track at North Head weaves its way round the point. Go left and take every opportunity to detour off the main track to peer over the edge at the boiling sea as it pounds the rocks below. The fencing is for your safety — don't climb over or around it, and supervise your children. There have been fatalities here.** Northwards up the coast is Blue Fish Point, a black spot for Sydney rock fishermen. Fishing is Australia's most

> *The long-nosed bandicoot, once abundant on North Head and up the northern peninsula, is now almost extinct. It has been listed as an endangered population. The small nocturnal marsupial's main predators are feral and domestic cats, dogs and foxes. Keep a lookout for their diggings which you might see at the round entrance to their nests. But just look, don't touch.*

deadly sport. Often anglers are washed off the rocks by a rogue wave, and then sucked under. Their bodies are not recovered for days. This popular spot is under the North Head Water Treatment Station, which makes for bumper fishing but treacherous and slippery conditions. You may notice the 'tide mark' out to sea — after treatment sewage is pumped 3.6 kilometres out to sea via the deep ocean outfall. When at the tip of North Head, if you look closely at the southern coastline, the dip just back from South Head is The Gap, Sydney's most famous suicide spot.

In 1980 North Head was barren — there was no flora here, and it was a favourite tip site. Hundreds of stolen cars were pushed off the cliffs and left to rust in the surf below. Most of the wrecks were recovered during a massive clean-up around the time the Fairfax Track was made. The National Parks and Wildlife Service planted some of the headland, and with natural regeneration over 600 plant species can now be found.

⑨ Go back down the road to the Quarantine Station in time for the 1.10 pm tour. The site at Spring Cove was chosen because of its isolation from Sydney Cove, its fresh water, the safe mooring in stormy weather and because it was difficult to escape from. Ship-owners initially resented quarantine since it cost them money to have their ships idle and they had to pay for their passengers while in quarantine. After Governor Darling's son died from whooping cough and another disease-ridden ship arrived without being quarantined, the Quarantine Act was passed in 1832 in a bid to stop disease spreading. Conditions were rough: quarantined passengers were put to work clearing bush, pitching their own tents and erecting permanent buildings including the hospital.

The station's inadequacies were highlighted with the arrival of the *Lady McNaughton* in 1837, on which 54 people died of typhus fever on the voyage and another 13 in quarantine. The doctor wrote to Governor Bourke that 'the scenes of misery, wretchedness and disease which everyone presented, were truly appalling'. The passengers were kept at the station for 11 weeks. Overcrowding was commonplace, with four children often sharing a hospital bed. The passengers did most of the work, the kitchens were primitive and many such basic amenities as toilets were missing.

Conditions eventually improved, and with them came a three-tier class system for the healthy. First-class passengers were allocated the best food and accommodation on shore — for which the shipping company paid

---

Surgeons were paid by the number of immigrants they landed alive. The fee: 20 shillings a head (around $150 today). And judging by their list of duties, they earned every penny. They were in charge of discipline, cleanliness, rations, sleeping arrangements and entertainment, to name but a few.

Half of Sydney's Aboriginal population was wiped out by smallpox within 12 months of the First Fleet's arrival, and the job was almost complete within seven years. Death moved so fast that very little was documented about the Kuringgai-speaking Aborigines of the North Shore. The burial or cremation ceremonies were dispensed with — bodies were left floating in the harbour or rotting in the bush. It's believed the Kayimai clan of about 50 or so lived around here, and they called the area Karrangla. The plentiful seafood was their staple diet, supplemented by plants, roots and small animals. They lived close to the shore, particularly in summer, their food source being more important to them than their accommodation. Their society started to break down with the arrival of the First Fleet. They had practically no resistance to the introduced diseases and had to compete with the Europeans for food.

— and were given access to one of Sydney's most exclusive harbourside beaches. Second-class passengers were only allowed to swim by invitation, and third class weren't allowed down to the beach at all.

In 1881 it was the Europeans' turn for a smallpox outbreak. A large number of locals were forcibly removed from their homes and quarantined at North Head, causing so much commotion that a Royal Commission was held, resulting in a rebuilding program at the station.

Bubonic plague was the next epidemic, and the station once again saw Sydneysiders interned. The plague's brush was so broad that many other areas of Sydney were used for isolation as well. One hundred graves were added to those at the station — all victims of the plague were buried here.

At the end of the First World War the Quarantine Station boasted 1130 beds, enough to

Controversy raged for decades over how the deadly smallpox germs were spread. The 'Miasmatics' believed germs were spread by gas or miasma generated by dying people, decaying organic matter, swamps and so on, and the 'Contagionists', who were proved to be right, believed the disease was spread from person to person. Inside the hospital there was an intricate ventilation system to stop the southerly winds blowing in one side and out the other, in theory to stop sending the deadly germs over to Manly.

The English practised their own form of smallpox prevention in the mid-18th century. By rubbing scabs into an open wound, or inhaling powdered scabs, a mild attack developed, hopefully generating long-lasting immunity to the disease. Unfortunately, this mild attack could sometimes develop into the real thing. It's thought this may be how the Aborigines became infected.

Thursday Island at the tip of Cape York Peninsula were improved; victims were taken off incoming ships and others were vaccinated so that by the time they reached Sydney their quarantine period was over. The *Nikko Maru* was the last ship to be quarantined in 1972. Cyclone Tracy refugees stayed at the station in 1975, followed by Vietnamese orphans a year later.

The most fascinating part of this tour is the rock engravings down at the wharf at Spring Cove. Hundreds of inmates recorded the ships they came on, their family names, the length of stay and some wry comments.

Either follow the map back to Manly wharf or catch the 135 bus, which should be waiting outside the Quarantine Station gates. If you want you can come back here at night for a Ghost Tour, also run by the National Parks and Wildlife Service.

cater for the biggest ocean liner. Soldiers returning home with Spanish flu were isolated here. Australia, the only country in the world to attempt maritime quarantine, was successful until let down by a neighbouring state. New South Wales police were placed on guard at the Victorian border to stop those infected with the virus from crossing over, but the damage had been done. The Royal Prince Alfred, Randwick and the Coast hospitals joined the Quarantine Station to nurse the flu victims.

In time, quarantine facilities on

WALK 15

BARRENJOEY LIGHTHOUSE TO PALM BEACH

START POINT:	Palm Beach Golf Course on Barrenjoey Road.
FINISH:	Ocean Place, Palm Beach.
HOW TO GET THERE:	By the 190 bus from Wynyard to Palm Beach Golf Course (recommended); or by ferry or jetcat from Circular Quay to Manly, then the 169 bus to Dee Why and change to the 190 bus at Palm Beach.
LENGTH:	5.25 kilometres (golf course to lighthouse and back 3.5 kilometres).
WALKING TIME:	40 minutes lighthouse only; 1.25 hours including Palm Beach.
ACTUAL TIME:	3 to 3.5 hours.
RATING:	The lighthouse track is a steep, uneven and rocky climb. There's a bit of bush whacking to get out to the Stewart Towers site. The Palm Beach section is flat and easy.
WEATHER CHECK:	Not recommended on a rainy day.
REFRESHMENTS:	Available at the seaplane base and at Palm Beach; nothing at the lighthouse.

Unsuitable for wheelchairs and strollers.

*t*his picturesque walk takes you up the most northern tip of Sydney, where the Pacific Ocean rolls in
on the eastern side, and the tranquil waters of
Pittwater stretch west on the other. Between these two
pieces of water lies beautiful sleepy Palm Beach with
its golden sand and multi -million dollar properties.
Reaching north across a sandy spit is the rugged
Barrenjoey headland and lighthouse with its spectacular views. This area is of historic importance — it was
named before Sydney, was a deadly peril to seafarers, a
haven for rum-runners and was once an island that
became joined to the mainland approximately 6000
years ago.

Governor Phillip named the headland Barrenjuee in
1788 just six weeks after arriving, when he came looking for arable land to feed his Port Jackson settlement.
Controversy over the spelling continued for almost two
centuries until it was finally agreed it should be
Barrenjoey, meaning small kangaroo in Aboriginal.
There is no evidence of the Aborigines actually living
on the headland, but it appears they did come in contact with Governor Phillip when he and Lieutenant
Bradley sailed by during their mission of discovery.

The steep climb up the rocky four-wheel drive track
takes you through an amazing range of natural vegetation. The walk ends with a stroll along Palm Beach's
glorious golden sands and a great view of the real
estate. And if you are feeling affluent, you can fly back
to Sydney in the seaplane.

*This walk is dedicated to Jervis and Bridget Sparks, tenants in
Cottage 2, Barrenjoey Lighthouse, and authors of* Tales From
Barrenjoey.

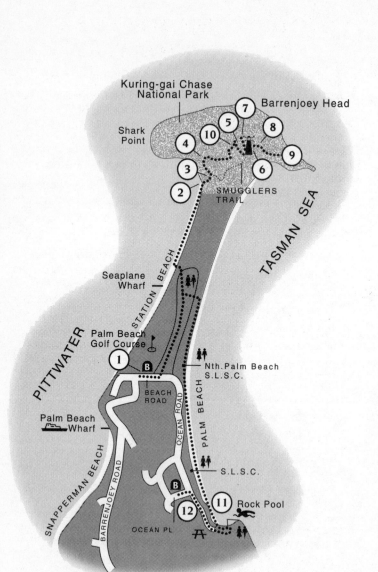

Kuring-gai Chase
National Park

Barrenjoey Head

Shark
Point

⑦
⑤
⑩
⑧
④
⑨
③
⑥
②

SMUGGLERS
TRAIL

TASMAN SEA

STATION BEACH

Seaplane
Wharf

Palm Beach
Golf Course

PITTWATER

①
Ⓑ

BEACH
ROAD

Nth. Palm Beach
S.L.S.C.

OCEAN ROAD

PALM BEACH

Palm Beach
Wharf

SNAPPERMAN BEACH

BARRENJOEY ROAD

Ⓑ

S.L.S.C.

⑫

⑪ Rock Pool

OCEAN PL

POINTS OF INTEREST ALONG THE WAY

① **Your bus stop is at the Palm Beach Golf Course, beside the entrance to Governor Phillip Park, where you turn left and head towards the lighthouse. Walk along the beach on Pittwater until you reach the rusty red shed and lighthouse signpost.**

② The shed was built from cast-off roofing iron from the lighthouse cottages by the grandson of the last lighthouse keeper. The other two cottages on your left were built by First World War diggers. Sydney acting legend and now movie director Mel Gibson made his first film here. *Tim* was shot at Doo Mee, the cottage on your right. The area also attracts wildlife visitors — grey-headed flying foxes from the Gordon colony flock to the huge Moreton Bay fig each February to feed, and there's a resident pair of foxes. Note the pocket of rainforest near the bottom of the track.

③ **Head off up the sandy track. About where it turns rocky, 30 metres short of a padlocked post in the middle of the road, are some hard-to-see rock steps on your right. They mark the entrance to the Smugglers' Trail.** Built in 1843 by convict boatmen, the trail leads to the lookout point on top of Barrenjoey. It was also used by the lighthouse keepers who

manned the original lights, the Stewart Towers, and who lived in cottages on the present-day golf course. If you're feeling energetic climb up Smugglers' Trail to the lighthouse — it's shorter, but steeper and rougher. Or come back that way.

④ The road you're on was built in 1880 to haul up materials for the current sandstone lighthouse. The dolphin in the rock by the locked post is not an

> The local Aborigines, who belonged to the Garigal clan of the Kuringgai-speaking tribe, made their canoes from Bangalay bark; scorching it, stripping it in one piece, then tying and gluing the ends. The fragile craft weren't suitable for Broken Bay's rough seas, and one early account said the canoes rode so low the Aborigines looked as if they were sitting in the sea. The Aborigines didn't live on Barrenjoey itself, but preferred the Palm Beach area and the calmer waters of Pittwater. Their staple diet of seafood and fish was plentiful until early settlement around Sydney Harbour forced many of those clans to move up here. The Garigals also didn't escape the ravages of smallpox and other diseases they had no immunity to, and their numbers were thought to have halved within the first year of white settlement.

Aboriginal carving but etched by a friend of one of the lighthouse keepers. Where the road sweeps sharply to the right, a colony of koalas was burnt to death in the 1967 bushfire. Now tawny frogmouths can be seen in the evening. The vegetation here has changed to open forest. The bangalay eucalypt, the gums with shiny green leaves and rough furrowed bark, are the most common species.

When you can catch a glimpse of the lighthouse and its cottages, notice the vegetation has changed again to denser, shorter, windswept heathland with banksias, wattles, tea-trees and the antisocial prickly hakeas. The tussock-like bushes with sweet-smelling spiky flowering stems were used by the Aborigines for basket-making. They also ground the seeds into flour. The lizards basking in the sun could be blue tongues, Cunningham skinks or long copper-tailed skinks.

⑤ The first building you come to is a sandstone semi. Cottage No. 2 is tenanted by Jervis and Bridget Sparks, who have spent the last 30 or so years faithfully restoring it, even though they don't own it. If their door is open pop in for a chat

Australia's first lighthouses used sperm whale oil, and before that a concoction of seal oil and coconut oil was trialled.

Local lore states that when rounding Barrenjoey Head, if you can see the lantern room railing, then you are safe; if not, you are in peril.

and check out their great collection of memorabilia. Next door cottages 1 and 3 are rented by mostly absent tenants, and then there is the present-day lighthouse, which incidentally is never open to the public. Joern Utzon, architect of the Sydney Opera House, claimed this cottage as his favourite Australian building because of its bull-nose sandstone. Each cottage, he said, was like an original oil painting — so different from its partner.

The first warning beacon on Barrenjoey was a fire lit in a basket during stormy weather in 1855. 1866 was a particularly bad one for shipwrecks. Two years later the Stewart Towers were built — two wooden structures, standing 700 metres apart, beaming a white light 13 kilometres out to sea. The case for an even stronger light was highlighted when the 'Dandenong Gale' roared through ten years later, its 245 kilometre an hour winds sinking the schooner *Industry* just off the headland.

⑥ The present-day sandstone lighthouse was built in 1880-81 at a cost of 13,695 pounds. The sandstone was quarried up here, and everything else was hauled up by horses along the trolley track from the jetty below.

The original lens, costing an extra 2210 pounds, is still shining today. It has survived numerous disastrous gales. In 1991 cricket ball-sized hail flung by 230 kilometre an hour winds punched holes through the lantern room windows. The lens survived, but the lamp didn't, leaving the lighthouse in darkness for two days. The original fixed red, non-flashing light could be seen 24 kilometres out to sea, and was fuelled by kerosene. In 1932 the light was changed to an automated white group flash with a radius of 40 kilometres. It was electrified in 1972, giving off the same candle power as 75 cars with their lights on high beam.

> *Smuggling liquor was big business in the early 19th century. Many a vessel escorted out of Port Jackson could be found selling their wares in these waters, especially as rum fetched 7 pounds a gallon, a little less than a month's wage for a lighthouse keeper. In 1843 the Customs Station was established (behind Doo Mee), and those chosen to watch and wait were called the 'coast waiters'. Hoping to scare duty evaders, cut-out replicas in full military dress could be seen atop Barrenjoey. Rumour has it one short-sighted traveller actually accosted a wooden redcoat when the lifeless sentry refused to doff his hat.*

(7) With the lighthouse at your back and the Gledhill Monument in front of you, take the rough track down about 20 metres until you come to a rock plateau looking out to sea. Sit and take in the uninterrupted view of Lion Island, Gosford and Brisbane Water. Famous Australian novelist Thomas Keneally wrote *Blood Red Sister Rose* on this very same rock.

(8) **Retrace your steps and again at the monument with Lion Island behind you, look left to a scruffy wire enclosure.** Keeper of the Stewart Towers and the present lighthouse, George Mulhall, and his wife Mary, are buried here. George's epitaph has a timely message. Local history says George was struck by lightning and burnt to a cinder, but his death certificate claims he died of apoplexy (stroke). Surely the lightning would have caused that! Lightning did strike his son George, badly burning his arm. George kept his arm wrapped in a snake skin after that to make sure lightning didn't strike twice! Vandals have made it even up here, hence the ugly mesh fence; likewise round the tower.

> The automatic light on Barrenjoey was stopped for several years during the Second World War and only used to guide convoys up the coast. The lighthouse also played a part in spreading the news when the First World War was over. The keeper's son picked up a semaphore or flag signal from a passing ship, and sprinted down to Palm Beach to tell the locals.

(9) **Continue eastward away from the lighthouse through the bush for about six minutes, along the most worn track. Near the cliff edge there's a cairn proclaiming the eastern site of the Stewart Towers. Make your way back along the same track, keeping the lighthouse in sight for a guide.**

(10) The trig station marking the western Stewart Tower and

Long before overland transport to Sydney, the first fresh vegetables for the city were grown here. They were rowed out through the surf and taken to town in work boats. An industrious Chinese firm carried on a prosperous fish-drying business near the present Palm Beach jetty. Ah Chuey paid 5 shillings a dozen for snapper; sometimes two or three boatloads would be piled up on Snapperman Beach waiting for an overnight cook-up.

the site of the first flagpole is just as difficult to find. Back down the four-wheel drive track about 100 metres on your right is a short, overgrown track. They're just in there.

Either go back down the four-wheel drive track, or down Smugglers' Trail leading off between the two cottages.

(11) **Walk back along the beach where you came in, turn left up past the toilet block, and right along the ridge between the ocean and Pittwater. Meander down the beautiful beach,** and stop for a bite to eat or a dip in the ocean pool at the end. The first attempt at the turn of the century to put the peninsula on the map failed dismally, with not a single sale. But the land was snapped up after a huge advertising campaign, even though there was still no direct road access from Sydney. The brochure read: 'Once a purchaser you'll probably remain the owner

— this land will quickly be too costly to replace.' How right they were. The ridge overlooking Palm Beach has been nicknamed 'Pill Hill' because of the number of doctors' holiday homes. About 70 per cent of dwellings remain weekenders with multi-million dollar price tags, fetching up to $6000 a week rental in summer.

(12) **Walk back to the bus stop up Ocean Place on your left, and catch the 190 back to Wynyard. Or catch the seaplane from the jetty on Station Beach.**

WALK 16

WEST
HEAD

START POINT:	Palm Beach wharf.
FINISH:	Palm Beach wharf.
HOW TO GET THERE:	Catch the 190 bus from Wynyard station to Palm Beach wharf and the ferry to Mackeral Beach.
LENGTH:	5 kilometres.
WALKING TIME:	1.75 hours.
ACTUAL TIME:	3.5 to 4 hours.
RATING:	This walk should not be attempted unless you are moderately fit. The track is single-file and rough, with several rock steps and steep sections, including a quite rugged climb to West Head. It's essential you take your own water, food, hat, sun screen and swimmers. Water containers can be refilled at West Head. There is unavoidable contact with the bush, so wear a long-sleeved shirt and trousers.
WEATHER CHECK:	This is not a wet weather walk as the paths would be too slippery.
REFRESHMENTS:	Food and drink available only at Palm Beach wharf, and water at West Head.

Unsuitable for wheelchairs and strollers.

*t*his is an extremely beautiful walk along the most northern tip of Sydney bushland in the Ku-ring-gai Chase National Park. The park's greatest drawcard is its rich Aboriginal sites. The Kuringgai-speaking Garigal clan lived here for thousands of years before the arrival of the First Fleet. They later regrouped and became known as the Broken Bay tribe, after their numbers were decimated by smallpox. You pass an overhang containing red and white hand stencils, which could date back 2000 years. This is Hawkesbury sandstone country where the most lasting examples of Aboriginal art can be found. The locals carved familiar objects such as fish, animals, boomerangs, mundoes or footprints, men hunting, and god-like figures. The large cave where Captain Phillip was offered shelter during his first trip to Pittwater is nestled in the rocks above beautiful Resolute Beach. The walk abounds with wildlife. There is a koala colony, swamp wallabies, green tree snakes hang from the canopy, and there's a cacophony of sounds and a blush of colour from the birdlife. There's the whole spectrum of Sydney bush — the tall Sydney red gums, blackbutts and turpentines, pockets of lush rainforest plus windswept heathland with sweet-smelling flowers. The view is spectacular — sheltered Pittwater flows to the south, named by Governor Phillip after British Prime Minister William Pitt the Younger. And from West Head Lion Island lies in the tranquil-looking but treacherous piece of water to the north that has claimed many a vessel and its crew. There are gun emplacements left over from the Second World War, still holding their positions.

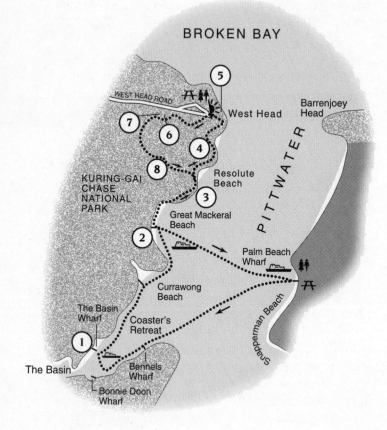

BROKEN BAY

WEST HEAD ROAD

⑤ West Head

Barrenjoey
Head

⑦

⑥

④

⑧

Resolute
Beach

③

Great Mackeral
Beach

KURING-GAI
CHASE
NATIONAL
PARK

②

Palm Beach
Wharf

Currawong
Beach

PITTWATER

The Basin
Wharf

Coaster's
Retreat

Snapperman Beach

①

The Basin

Bennels
Wharf

Bonnie Doon
Wharf

POINTS OF INTEREST ALONG THE WAY

① **Catch the ferry to Mackeral Beach, but first you will drop in at the Basin on your way.** Coasters Retreat, a sleepy little inlet was where the 'coasters' — the crudely built boats that ferried fresh food to Sydney — sheltered waiting for calm weather to make the 15 kilometre open sea trip. They gathered in groups here, hoping safety in numbers would stop them being pirated by escaped convicts trying to flee the colony. Coasters Retreat was also dubbed Smugglers Cove — large quantities of illegal liquor were smuggled in for local consumption or for shipment through Lane Cove to Sydney. Keg parties here were known to last three days, a big drink as smuggled rum cost an exorbitant 3 pounds a gallon. Long before the Europeans settled here, the local Aborigines roamed these shores, living off the sea and the bush, and moving on as food sources dictated. Aboriginal middens, or seafood kitchens, are dotted throughout Kur-ring-gai Chase, evidence of their long inhabitation here. At the Basin, as Coasters is now called, there are middens metres deep here still, but much deeper ones were destroyed when the early settlers mined the shells for lime. One year after white settlement Aboriginal numbers had been halved by the smallpox epidemic. Harbourside tribes were pushed northwards, and the Europeans were using traditional Aboriginal land to grow food. Competition for survival became so intense the Aborigines petitioned Governor Hunter for their own fishing grounds.

Coasters Retreat takes a place in constitutional Australian history, being host to the law makers who helped shape Australia as a nation. The retreat is remembered in history as the 'Lucinda Weekend', Easter 1891, when three colonial statesmen met on board the Queensland Government yacht Lucinda to nut out the contentious issues facing the preparation of the Australian Constitution. Being too rough at sea, the Lucinda put into Broken Bay for the weekend and spent Saturday night at the Basin, where there's little doubt the three men broke the deadlock over the thorny issues.

② **Get off the ferry at Mackeral Beach, turn right at the end of the jetty and walk to the end of the beach. You may have to ford a stream. Climb up the rocks beside two big palms and onto the track. Head off to the right with the sea beneath you.**

Once you have found your footing, keep your eyes peeled for koalas in the trees above. The colony was saved during the 1994 bushfires by the initiative of National Parks and Wildlife ranger Andrew Marshall. He burnt a firebreak around the colony, saving it from certain death. He didn't do the grass trees a favour, however, their stout black stumps being fire resistant. Black boys, one of the oldest plants in the world, were of great use to the Aborigines, yielding resin, nectar, nutritious starch, grubs, firesticks and fishing spears. The palm-like burrawangs were also a great food source, after the long process of soaking, grinding and baking to remove the poison. Early settlers and explorers alike were poisoned by the pineapple-like nut after roasting the bitter taste away, but not the toxin.

③ After about 15 minutes' walking there's a Garigal sign pointing up the hill. Keep going straight about 20 metres to the Resolute Beach sign, and then go down. Resolute Beach was named after the paddle-steamer *Resolute*, which ran aground but was towed free before breaking up on this beautiful beach. It was here that

Governor Phillip made first contact with the Aborigines while looking for suitable land to feed the masses at Port Jackson. A friendly old man and a boy showed them the best place to land, brought them fire, and showed them where they could shelter in a wide cave. The pair followed Phillip around in the rain the next day, and a woman showed him how to make a fishing hook. Phillip noticed many of the Broken Bay women had the first joint of the little finger on their left hand cut off, apparently to help them fish. The cabbage tree palms seen down here were eaten as a vegetable by the natives, but the tree died when the centre was removed.

Climb back up to the track and follow the West Head signs. All sorts of wildlife can be found in the national park, including snakes. They will normally slide off before you can come near, but treat them with respect. They don't like being cornered or trodden on. Of the poisonous variety there are brown, red-bellied black, yellow belly, death adder and black snakes, and the non-poisonous snakes are the whip, rock python, green python and green tree snake.

④ About ten minutes further on, keep an eye out on your right for a concrete fortification perched down the hill. Climb down and have a look. At the outbreak of the Second World War the rush was on to build mil-

itary defences on West Head. The military observation post on Barrenjoey Head was closed and

> In July 1942, a diary entry dramatically recorded a white wake proceeding downstream at 2 knots. Batteries opened fire and made a direct hit, but there was no sign of wreckage. The next day a giant turtle was washed ashore, apparently killed by a two-pounder!

West Head and Juno Point became the front line of defence. Two 4.7 inch guns were positioned in concrete emplacements at water level, and machine gun, observation and searchlight posts were also built to detect the arrival of the enemy. An anti-submarine net was stretched from Barrenjoey to West Head to prevent an underwater invasion.

Four minutes from here there's a turn-off to another beautiful beach. Go down the track if you want, but the distance and time are not added in to those given for this walk. The trees around here are much taller, stretching skyward for light and forming an overhead canopy. Also take time to look up at the amazing cliff formation and the overhangs.

Just before you climb the steps on the left, look for the rock orchids on the back of the huge rock on your right. The Aborigines roasted and ate orchid tubers, which are easiest to find when in flower in spring. You're now climbing up through a pocket of rainforest, which thrives on the existence of permanent water. Look out for native grapes — they look just like cultivated ones. The Aborigines ate them, but they are astringent and leave you with a dry mouth. Another fruit in abundance here is the purple lilly pilly, a favourite with the Aborigines and popular with the early settlers for making jam.

Follow the West Head sign, and climb down over the rock face. Notice the contortions of the Sydney red gum as you climb over its root in the creek. Watch out for the native sasparilla vine winding its way through the trees and acting as a trip wire for the unwary. Its elongated heart-shaped leaves were used as a tea and had many other medicinal purposes. The early settlers used it as a preventative against scurvy — it contains as much vitamin C as tomatoes. If you hear a crashing in the bush it could be a swamp wallaby, or two or three, dark in colour with a white tip on their tail. Stay still and wait for them to move again. Their numbers are increasing after the 1994 bushfire.

After this big climb, look for a rock ledge on your right for a superb view down to Pittwater and across to the Barrenjoey Lighthouse. The Barrenjoey headland was once an island and became joined to the mainland through the formation of a tombolo or sandspit at the end of the last ice age, about 6000 years ago.

⑤ **Rejoin the track and within minutes you will be at West Head lookout. Take a breather here, refill your water bottles, and use the facilities.** Watch out for the big black goannas with their spectacular yellow-spotted legs and bands around their bodies hunting for scraps. They eat just about anything, are plentiful in this area, and can grow to about 2 metres. Lion Island, the one that looks like its namesake, was first called Mount Elliot after the northern end of Gibraltar Rock. This peaceful-looking piece of water is treacherous, being responsible for many shipwrecks and the loss of many lives. Vessels seeking refuge in Broken Bay were unaware they would have been safer at sea. Five bodies of water converge at Lion Island and the force can be so strong it can make an anchored boat spin like a top. This area was also the feeding ground for large sharks, as poor Captain Lusk found out when his coaster *Hazard* was wrecked in a storm. All that remained of him was his head! The meshing of Sydney beaches has greatly reduced the shark population, and the waterway tamed somewhat by the controlling of floodwaters at Warragamba Dam. On a more tranquil note, there's a fairy penguin colony on Lion Island. They breed in safety there, where nobody is allowed to land.

Cross the picnic area towards the car park, and take the Red Hands Trail. About ten minutes on keep a lookout on your right for a sandstone overhang with a seat in it. The red colour, iron oxide, is leeched out of the rock by rising water, leaving porous white sandstone with a hard crust.

⑥ **At the 'T' intersection turn left, and then on your right is the hand stencil cave.** The stencils are barely visible now, so please don't touch. The white hand stencils were usually made by a hand greased with animal fat held against the rock and a mixture of white pipeclay and water was blown on from the artist's mouth. Red stencils were made the same way, but often human or animal blood was added. The significance of this artform isn't really known; it's believed some hand stencils were made to form a living spiritual link with a dead relative.

Continue on the track, noticing the trees are getting smaller and the bush is getting more scrubby. **At the 'T', turn left onto the four-wheel drive track,** where the bush has now shortened and become exposed heathland to cope with the hot dry conditions. Look for the pretty grevilleas — the Aborigines soaked the flowers in water for a sweet drink — the mountain devils with their red seed pods, and the soft flannel flowers. Over 900 plant species survive in this arid climate.

(7) **About five minutes down the four-wheel drive track is an Aboriginal engraving site. This is a sacred site, and the engravings will last a lot longer if you don't walk on them. About 18 metres from the sign, towards the ocean and in front of a bottlebrush, is the fish. On your right, 10 metres back towards the track from the Headland Track sign, are the eels and the man.** The artist would draw the subject with ochre or a stick, then punch a series of holes around the outline. Sometimes the engraving would be left like this, but usually it was filled in. Successive generations had to re-groove the engravings to keep contact with the Dreamtime. After the arrival of the Europeans, women in dresses and sailing ships appeared in Aboriginal engravings.

Leave the front of the site via the Headland Track, and stay left when it rejoins the four-wheel drive track. About 12 minutes from the engraving site there's a plaque explaining which plants and trees the local Aborigines made use of. Not far from here, take the next left turn down the stone steps.

(8) **This supposedly is the cave or overhang** where the old Aboriginal man and the boy wanted to bring Governor Phillip that cold wet night in March 1788. As you can see there would have been plenty of room for everyone.

Phillip apparently paid for his ingratitude towards this hospitable offer, as he suffered bad back for the rest of his life from spending so much time sleeping in boats and on beaches in bad weather. But there was one bonus — the 50-year-old Phillip had one front tooth missing, which stood him in good stead with the local Aborigines. During part of their initiation ceremony, young Aboriginal boys had a front tooth punched out, so perhaps they thought Phillip had undergone an initiation of his own!

Walk down the hundreds of steps through the casuarina forest and turn right onto the path you came up on just before Resolute Beach. Walk back along the beach to the wharf, and catch the ferry back to Palm Beach. From there you can return to Wynyard station by bus.

WALK 17

ROSE BAY TO NIELSEN PARK

START POINT:	Bay View Lane, Rose Bay.
FINISH:	Nielsen Park, Vaucluse.
HOW TO GET THERE:	Catch the 324 or 325 bus from Circular Quay or Elizabeth Street and get off at Kincoppal Rose Bay Convent. Or take the Bondi Junction train from Town Hall to Edgecliff and connect with those buses to Rose Bay.
LENGTH:	A little over 3 kilometres.
WALKING TIME:	1–2 hours.
ACTUAL TIME:	The whole day if you stop to enjoy the views and rest a while at Nielsen Park or Vaucluse House.
RATING:	Some rugged terrain and uneven stone steps along the Hermitage Foreshore, but from there the path is concrete and even.
WEATHER CHECK:	Should it rain heavily, trees are your only shelter until you arrive at Nielsen Park or Vaucluse House.
REFRESHMENTS:	A picnic lunch is suggested. The kiosk at Nielsen Park is not always open. The area is especially lovely towards sunset on a balmy summer evening, so take a picnic dinner.

Unsuitable for wheelchairs and strollers.

Wrapped around some of eastern Sydney's loveliest bays and quiet residential beaches is a 1 kilometre waterside bush track called the Hermitage Foreshore. It's a peaceful stretch of Sydney Harbour National Parkland tucked in between luxurious homes. These are ancient Aboriginal fishing coves, rich in examples of how and where this area's original inhabitants lived. When Governor Arthur Phillip asked these locals where they came from, they said 'Eora', which means 'here — this land'. The name stuck and Sydney's tribe was called Eora. The sub-tribe, or clan, that lived along these beaches were called Cadigal. The Rose Bay to Shark Bay foreshore was laden with middens (leftover shells from countless meals of fish and seafood), proof that the Hermitage Track was a place of great importance to the Cadigals. They set out in canoes from here, slept in the overhanging rocks and carved drawings into the rocks at Milk Beach. After the Hermitage Track you'll come to Nielsen Park, also known as Shark Beach. Nielsen Park is one of Sydney's oldest and most popular recreational areas and comes complete with a shark net and charming 1914 dressing sheds, so you can shower after a well-deserved dip at the halfway point. The beach was initially owned by a wealthy colonial who was forced to hand his choice land back to the government because the people thought it unfair that only the rich had access to the harbour foreshore. We'll visit Vaucluse House and look more closely at William Charles Wentworth's life, together with the Aboriginal people that roamed these romantic inlets.

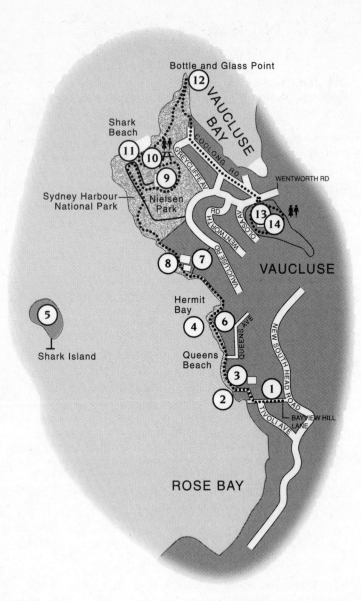

Bottle and Glass Point

⑫

VAUCLUSE BAY

Shark Beach

COOLONG RD

⑪ ⑩ ⑨

GREYCLIFFE AV

WENTWORTH RD

Sydney Harbour National Park

Nielsen Park

WENTWORTH RD

GLOSSOP AV

⑬ ⑭

VAUCLUSE

⑧ ⑦

VAUCLUSE RD

Hermit Bay

④ ⑥

QUEENS AV

NEW SOUTH HEAD ROAD

⑤

Shark Island

Queens Beach

③

①

②

BAYVIEW HILL LANE

TIVOLI AVE

ROSE BAY

POINTS OF INTEREST
ALONG THE WAY

(1) Get off the bus at Kincoppal Rose Bay Convent and walk to the bottom of Bay View Lane for a good view of Rose Bay. The first white men to live here were convicts who set up a salt boilers' factory on the beach in 1805. This is the widest bay in Sydney Harbour and when its land was first advertised for sale, the advertisement read 'the very first amphitheatre for bathing in the world'. The beach was originally a huge tidal mudflat that was reclaimed in 1902, and the seawall was added in 1924.

(2) Follow the signs to the Hermitage Reserve. Our walk begins with the track at the very end of Bay View Lane. You'll soon notice that seaplanes take off from Rose Bay, a historic launching pad that dates back to a 1938 flying boat base. During the Second World War it became an RAAF base and later the Sydney Water Airport for Qantas flights carrying people to the United Kingdom. The small planes you see now are doing chartered joy-flights for tourists. **After some distance you'll come**

> *Rose Bay was a battleground for the Cadigal Aboriginal people. They called the bay* Pan-ner-rong, *which means 'blood'.*

> *The Aboriginal women of Port Jackson (Sydney Harbour) were all missing the little finger of their left hand. String was tied tightly around the finger's lower joint when they were babies. This procedure was called* mal gun. *The joint would eventually fall off, later helping a grown Cadigal woman handle her fishing hook and line without tangling it up in her fingers. The Port Jackson men were without a right front tooth. It was knocked out during an initiation ceremony.*

(3) across the Kincoppal Rose Bay Convent cemetery on your right. In 1882 five nuns of the Society of the Sacred Heart came to Sydney and chose this land to establish their school. The convent was designed by John Horbury Hunt and built in 1885. Just near the cemetery's fence is a Celtic cross — a tribute to the convent's founder, Reverend Mother Febronie Vercruysse. She died in England in 1895. **Soon you'll come across Queens Beach.**

(4) Tiny Hermit Bay was the perfect hideaway for the convicts turned hermits who built their shacks here in the early 1800s. When it was Cadigal territory, the Aboriginal people slept and ate around these overhanging rocks. Here the men stalked fish with four-pronged spears, tipped with sharpened animal or fish bones. Strips of bark were used to make fishing canoes and cooking vessels, and they would also fill the bark with soil to make a smoky fire for their catch.

5. The water here teemed with sharks in the 1800s. Many locals mistakenly believe this tiny outcrop won its name because of its shark-like shape, but it's because sharks were so prevalent here. When whaling outside the heads was popular, sharks would follow the whaling boats around the harbour. If you threw in a line now, you'd be more likely to pull in a flathead, whiting, bream or leatherjacket. Shark Island, known as Bo-a-millie to the Cadigals, is the third deepest location in the harbour.

6. From the other side of Hermit Bay you can see the green-tiled roof and cream gables of this walk's namesake, the Hermitage. This house is probably the oldest on the foreshore. It was built in 1837, and enlarged in 1868, in 1936 and again in 1964.

7. **The track proceeds to an open area where three buildings are nestled in a grassy glade.** The mansion furthest north, or the far left, is Carrara. Inside there is a series of fireplaces made from Italian Carrara marble. Outside, the stone was quarried from the surrounding beaches. Sydney's first elected mayor built Carrara in the

From 1827 most of the Hermitage foreshore belonged to William Charles Wentworth. His mother was a convict (for theft) and his father a doctor of poor, but well-connected Yorkshire lineage. In 1813 Wentworth, along with Blaxland and Lawson, found a way over the Blue Mountains, west of Sydney. He then studied law at Cambridge, returned to Sydney with his degree, and became the colony's most prominent politician, calling himself the First Australian. He helped draft the constitution for a self-governing New South Wales.

1850s. The surrounding 5 hectare property is now known as Strickland House and in 1915 it was dedicated to new mothers and seriously ill women. Now the buildings are empty, with only the ground floor used for weddings and private parties. On the hill beyond Carrara to the north is a two-storey stone coach house and stables that doubled as the mansion's servants' quarters in the 1800s. Feel free to wander around.

8. **Tingara and Milk Beach front Strickland House.** When the main form of transport and delivery was by boat, milk was delivered via the beach and so Milk Beach gained its name. Its milky-white sand also contributed to its name. Fish and shield figures were carved by the Cadigals onto the rocks here. The rocks are known as one of the best carving sites in the district

because much of the art work is protected by a covering of water and sand. They are exposed only after heavy rain, and at low tide.

⑨ The Hermitage Track restarts at the northern end

When W.C.Wentworth's eldest daughter Thomasine (known as Timmie) married in 1844, he gave her the Milk Beach land as a wedding present. But Timmie's new husband had deviously planned to marry her with the intention of forcing her to cut all family ties. The alienation devastated the Wentworths — they had no idea that Thomas Fisher would force Timmie to break off all social contact with her family once she had married him.

of Milk Beach. After about 100 metres the track takes you up wooden stairs into Nielsen Park's 21 hectares. Turn left at the bitumen service road and follow it around to the right where you'll soon see Greycliffe House. This 1852 Victorian Gothic home is nicknamed 'the Doll's House'. John Hilly designed Greycliffe House for Wentworth's third eldest child, Fanny, whose husband John Reeve bought the land off his father-in-law in 1850. When the land reverted to the public purse, it became a hospital for babies with gastro-enteritis and in 1938, the Tresillian Training Centre for Mothercraft. Since 1978 it's been part of the Sydney Harbour National Park and is now an office of the National Parks and Wildlife Service.

(10) **From Greycliffe House walk towards the beach** and its 1920s kiosk. The 1930s changing sheds are just inland of the kiosk. In later years visitors would nude sunbathe in the separate male and female sheds.

(11) **Walk up the beach's promenade** and on your right, next to the kiosk, you'll see a semi-circular concrete bench with a memorial plaque dedicated to William Albert Notting. Together with Neil Nielsen, after whom the park was named, Notting was the power and driving force behind the Harbour Foreshores Vigilance Committee. In the early 1900s this group pushed for all the privately owned Sydney Harbour bushlands to be returned to the public. By 1912 all of Wentworth's land was signed over to the government. **Have a rest and a swim here.**

(12) **Walk to the promenade's northern end to stone steps behind the men's toilets. The steps lead you onto a bitumen service road and towards Vaucluse Point.** The views are fantastic from here. Veer left off the road and go to the right of the point where you can see Bottle and Glass Rocks. This rocky outcrop was called *Moring* by the Cadigals, but white settlers renamed it after its resemblance to a glass and a bottle. **Go back to the service road and follow it until you reach Coolong Road.**

(13) Off Wentworth Road is Vaucluse House. **Follow the signs to 'House Entry'**. Vaucluse House began as a small cottage built by Irish kidnapper Sir Henry Brown Hayes. He bought the Vaucluse estate in 1803 and gave it the French name meaning 'closed valley'. Hayes was transported to Australia for abducting a young heiress and forcing her to marry him. In 1797 Cork newspapers reported Hayes hired men to hold up her carriage and carry her off to his home. A priest did his best to recite the wedding vows, but Mary Pike would have none of it. Within days she was rescued by friends. The 35-year-old Hayes went into hiding, but re-emerged two years later. Condemned to death for the scam, his sentence was commuted to transportation for life. He was short, pock-skinned and terrified of snakes. He so believed in the snake-free virtues of Irish soil he imported and surrounded the house with 50 tonnes of it.

(14) William Wentworth bought Vaucluse House after seeing the advertisement of 'a genteel dwelling with eight rooms'. He added many more rooms and the outhouses still standing today. He and his wife Sarah filled it with ten children and European furniture. In 1853 Wentworth followed the Constitution Bill that he'd helped draft to London. By the time of his death in 1872, he had ensured all Australians were protected by trial by jury, the right to hold public meetings and free speech. When his body was brought back to Australia, 60,000 people watched his state funeral pass from the city to the family tomb on Chapel Road. Sadly, Sarah's body was never returned to her beloved Vaucluse House.

The bus stop to take you back to Town Hall station is right outside Vaucluse House.

THE GAP, SOUTH HEAD

START POINT:	Watsons Bay wharf.
FINISH:	Watsons Bay wharf.
HOW TO GET THERE:	The most pleasant way to get to Watsons Bay is by ferry from Circular Quay, however timetables are sketchy. Buses 324 and 327, also from the quay, are more reliable.
LENGTH:	3 kilometres.
WALKING TIME:	2 hours.
ACTUAL TIME:	Less than an hour if you don't stop too long for the views.
RATING:	Moderate; some unsealed, uneven ground and steps.
WEATHER CHECK:	No protection from rain after Watsons Bay.
REFRESHMENTS:	There are cafes and restaurants at Watsons Bay, though they're not always open. A picnic lunch is recommended for your destination at South Head.

Unsuitable for wheelchairs and strollers.

Watsons Bay and the rugged cliffs behind it are called The Gap. The cliffs come to a tip of land called South Head, which is opposite North Head, and together they form the entrance to Sydney Harbour. This harbour gateway is notoriously tricky to navigate, and subsequently shipwrecks litter the coastline. The walk from The Gap to South Head through Watsons Bay is packed with some of Sydney's most incredible views and a unique history. This is where the first settlers finally set foot on what was to become Sydney soil. We'll cover the culture of this early isolated fishing village and discover an Aboriginal sub-tribe, the Cadigal. They moved in small groups and were one of the first clans to disappear. English diseases and territory ownership wiped out the Cadigals within the first five years of Sydney's foundation. The area developed into a cosy and somewhat jolly village, where holiday-makers traditionally go to enjoy the sun on the peaceful beaches. The walk culminates at South Head after a coastal bush track past the First World War gunneries and naval fortifications. You'll pass four small beaches, one of them nude (though you can pass Lady Bay Beach without a glimpse of the bathers because it's nestled behind a bush track).

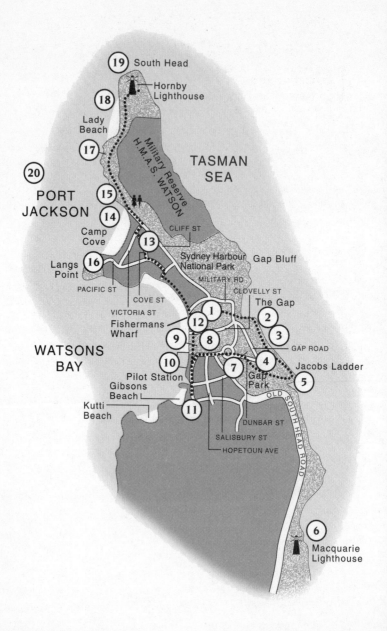

POINTS OF INTEREST ALONG THE WAY

① Your start point is Robertson Park, between the ocean and Watsons Bay. Robert Watson was a local Englishman who worked as the harbourmaster in 1811. Most of the other Anglo-Saxon names around here remain from those who built their homes from 1792 to the 1830s. Today the locals often refer to the area as Watto Bay. Down the centre of the park you can see a slight incline formed by a freshwater creek which supplied early settlers and the Cadigals with their water.

② Take the diagonal path that runs through the park from Watsons Bay wharf to the hidden cliffs opposite. The old inn near the stairs to The Gap is famous for its dog. The canny canine had a sixth sense for suicide and would bark non-stop when someone was up here contemplating the leap. There is no other location in Australia that has such a strange reputation for suicide. Every year 20 to 30 people take their own lives by jumping off The Gap. Unfortunately, about 100 people a year slip off, so explore at your peril. **Once at the top of the stairs** you can see how the waves have eaten this cliff area away, leaving a 'gap' in the cliffs, giving it its name. Experts say the ocean will eventually wear the gap completely through and in millions of years

this area will become an island. South Head's sister North Head is clearly visible across the Tasman Sea. On your left to the north is a rocky outcrop called Gap Bluff. All the bushland behind and around it is owned by the Royal Australian Navy. Called HMAS *Watson*, sailors and officers are trained in submarine and surface warfare here. The white building with the red roof is one of their many accommodation and training structures.

③ Continue south (your right if you're looking out to sea) up the path to the *Dunbar*'s anchor, which belonged to an elegant British clipper. In 1857 the *Dunbar* was bringing many locals home from England when it sank near here while trying to find the harbour entrance. Gale-force winds slammed the *Dunbar* up against the rocks; 121 people died. There was only one survivor, found clinging to a ledge near here.

④ In times of war, Gap Park was one of Sydney's most important 'tactical positions'. An 1870 Royal Commission decided to guard the harbour entrance with gun pits at outer (here) and inner South Head. The plant life around you now is mainly coastal heath, bottlebrush, tea-tree and callistemons.

⑤ **Jacob's Ladder is the crevice in the cliffs about 70 metres further along the path.** Up until a few decades ago rope ladders would hang straight down the cliff face here so fishermen could climb to the rocks below. The name came from a similarly designed ladder in the Old Testament.

⑥ **If you want to poke your nose just above the steps, they lead up to Old South Head Road and the Macquarie Lighthouse, Australia's oldest.** This area has been recorded as a Cadigal sacred site as for thousands of years it was their burial ground. Early observations indicate the Cadigals' methods for caring for their dead depended on the age of the deceased person: the elderly were cremated and the young were placed in a grass-lined grave and covered with soil. A lighthouse superintendent in 1800 recalls a young Aboriginal boy called Nanbarry who would rather stay the night in the lighthouse than face a

roaming long-gone ancestor outside. On another day come back for the bicentennial cliff walk, which continues past the lighthouse for just over a kilometre.

⑦ **At Jacob's Ladder, turn right down the path opposite. At the bottom of the gully you'll come to Dunbar Street. Turn left and head for the corner of Military Road.** On your right is the old town hall, once home to a man who lost his entire family in the *Dunbar* tragedy. It was also, among other things, the Watsons Bay Village Cinema, complete with open-air roof for the silent movie era.

⑧ **Head towards the roundabout where Military Road joins Old South Head Road. Go straight ahead down towards Marine Parade.** Coming up on your right is the grand old Dunbar House — a home, hotel, council chambers and finally a restaurant. In 1859 Henry Billings set up his zoo here, complete with tigress, grizzly bear and elephant. When he died, his wife's plea for government assistance to keep the zoo going went unheard, so she poisoned all 18 animals.

⑨ The obelisk on the corner of Marine Parade is a mystery monument, unofficially erected by the soldiers who built Old South Head Road and extended it all the way down this hill. From the mid-1840s Sydney's rich built their homes overlooking this area. Apparently the cottage own-

ers below called them the 'up-hillers', while they themselves were nicknamed the 'down-hillers'.

⑩ Past the Vaucluse Yacht Club and the Baths is the Watsons Bay Pilot Station — the big building with a wharf. This is the historical and current home of the harbour's bravest seafaring men — the pilots. Every day about ten enormous vessels come in and out of Port Jackson (Sydney Harbour). A pilot's job is to take over the international tankers' and cruise liners' navigation to bring them safely into Sydney's major wharves. Some of these boats weigh 70,000 tonnes and are almost three football fields long. The pilots leave from here on board 'pilot boats', which pull up alongside the huge ships

so the pilot can grab a flimsy ladder and board the ship. Pilots have left from this station to board vessels unfamiliar with the harbour since 1792.

⑪ Walk beyond the Pilot Station to Gibsons Beach. At the rear of this calm, sandy shoreline is a remarkable example of where the Cadigal clan lived. The Aborigines called the beach *Kooti*. They fished here and slept in the overhanging caves. The remnants of meals shared by these small nomadic family units are left in middens up and down these beaches. In 1805, only 17 years after settlement, an edition of the Sydney *Gazette* reported the natives had resorted to 'stealing' food. Robert Watson's small plantation of maize was raided and cleaned out by Aborigines.

(12) **Head back along the shoreline underneath the enormous fig trees** where rainbow lorikeets and rosellas frantically feed at sunset. Pass Fishermans Wharf and the famous Doyles Seafood Restaurant, where you'll find some **stairs at the end of Watsons Bay beach.**

(13) **Along leafy Cove Street** is a park that was once a swampy reservoir called the Wild Duck Pool.

(14) **Turn right into Victoria Street and left into Cliff Street for Camp Cove.** This is said to be the landing place of the First Fleet. After finding no fresh water at Botany Bay (which was also too shallow and sandy for good anchorage), Governor Arthur Phillip set off to explore Port Jackson, spotted back in 1770 by Captain Cook. When the three small boats rounded South Head they recorded finding a beach where they could anchor and cook a meal. Historians agree the beach was Camp Cove. An officer of the party diarised the Cadigal men did not give the white men a warm welcome. He wrote that the natives positioned themselves along the overhanging cliffs to your right and shook their spears. Others recorded that the Cadigals yelled 'warra-warra-warra', which means 'go away'.

(15) **Climb up the wooden steps furthest to your right and keep to the coastal path.** You are now on Sydney Harbour National Park land. This is also one of Sydney's most popular diving sites. Hundreds of seahorses and pipe fish breed here in August and September. Offshore towards the right is the remains of the city's first wharf.

(16) Look back towards the other end of the beach at the last house, almost on Green Point. This was Australia's first marine biological research station, occu-

pied by Russian scientist Baron Nicolai Miklouho-Maclay. Now it's a home for visiting defence personnel.

(17) **Walk up the path to what's called the Inner Battery:** gun pits that date back to 1873. Two war scares around 1853 and 1854, the Crimean and Russian wars, prompted the Australian Army into taking fortifications and defence more seriously. Five guns were mounted here so they could fire across Watsons Bay should someone sneak in the Heads. The guns were briefly mobilised in 1914 for the First World War, but most were destroyed after that. The area was used to move military goods off the old Camp Cove wharf during the Second World War. Under your feet is an intricate series of secret tunnels that lead from the cliffs to HMAS *Watson*.

(18) **Turn left at the bitumen service road, which will lead you past Lady Bay Beach.** Naked bathers have put up a good fight for their nude beaches. There are three in Sydney Harbour: Lady Bay, Obelisk (the little beach directly opposite this one) and Cobblers at Middle Head.

(19) A lookout station was established at South Head as early as 1790. Hunger and excitement at the arrival of a ship from the motherland made sure a fire was lit to alert the settlement supplies were coming. The stone

house is an old lighthouse keeper's residence, later serving as storage space for the navy. Beside it is Hornby Lighthouse. Both were built after the 1857 loss of the *Dunbar*.

(20) At low tide you can see the Sydney Harbour channel is divided in two by an outcrop of rocks called the Sow and Pigs. The rocks are marked with buoys and poles to warn boats of the danger. From here you also have a spectacular view of North Head, Manly Cove and Middle Head.

Walk back to Camp Cove the way you came, and cross the beach (for a change of scenery) to Green Point for the Pacific Street route back to The Gap and the bus stop or wharf. Catch the same buses, or ferry, back to the city.

WALK 19

PADDINGTON

START POINT:	Taylor Square, Oxford Street, Paddington.
FINISH:	Corner of Underwood and Oxford streets, Paddington.
HOW TO GET THERE:	Catch the 380 or 382 bus from Circular Quay and get off at Taylor Square.
LENGTH:	About 3 kilometres.
WALKING TIME:	2 hours.
ACTUAL TIME:	Allow about 3 hours to take in the sights.
RATING:	Easy: a well-surfaced, inner-city residential stroll.
WEATHER CHECK:	If it starts to rain Oxford Street is lined with fascinating shops to browse.
REFRESHMENTS:	Some cafes are open all day, others until 11 pm. This walk is highly recommended for a Saturday when you can finish at Paddington Markets.

Suitable for wheelchairs and strollers, with a lot of effort.

*P*addington holds many things for many people. For some it's the gay corner of Sydney, where men in sequins dance down the street in the Gay and Lesbian Mardi Gras. For others, Paddington has a Ye Olde England feeling, because of its 160-year-old houses. Then again, many people like Paddington for the thousands upon thousands of terraces that line its pretty, but oddly shaped streets. Paddo's earliest records show it wasn't good farmland, but water flowed freely from three creeks and a waterfall cascaded down to the swamplands of Rushcutters Bay. Settlement really began when the government decided new military quarters would be built on a sandy wasteland behind Paddington on South Head Road (now Oxford Street). A busy village was established and businesses and craftspeople flourished as the government constructed Victoria Barracks. Those workers' cottages are now some of Sydney's oldest homes. This walk leads you to them, sticking only to Paddington's most historic sites. Among the sites are the first colonial mansions, built by merchant princes who sold off their huge land grants and divided the land into countless parcels. These days the 4000 terraces are dotted with art galleries, restaurants and trendy shops. This stroll zigzags you past them, to take in all the best spots.

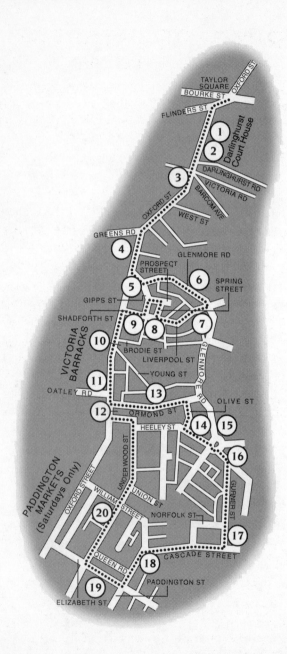

TAYLOR SQUARE
OXFORD ST
BOURKE ST
FLINDERS ST
①
②
Darlinghurst Court House
③
DARLINGHURST RD
VICTORIA RD
OXFORD ST
BARCOM AVE
WEST ST
GREENS RD
④
GLENMORE RD
PROSPECT STREET
⑥
SPRING STREET
GIPPS ST
⑤
SHADFORTH ST
⑨ ⑧
⑦
VICTORIA BARRACKS
⑩
BRODIE ST
LIVERPOOL ST
GLENMORE RD
⑪
YOUNG ST
OATLEY RD
⑬
OLIVE ST
⑫
ORMOND ST
HEELEY ST
⑭ ⑮
⑯
PADDINGTON MARKETS (Saturdays Only)
UNDER WOOD ST
UNION ST
GURNER ST
OXFORD STREET
WILLIAM STREET
⑳
NORFOLK ST
⑰
QUEEN RD
CASCADE STREET
⑱
PADDINGTON ST
⑲
ELIZABETH ST

POINTS OF INTEREST ALONG THE WAY

① **Start your walk at Taylor Square,** in front of Darlinghurst Supreme Court. Built between 1822 and 1885, the courthouse and the gaol behind it were originally called the Woolloomooloo Stockade. Over the years thousands came here to see 77 public hangings, the last one in 1907. Convicts were moved out to Long Bay Gaol in 1912 and the gaol's interior has been redesigned to house the East Sydney Campus of the Sydney Institute of Technology. Murder trials are still held in the courthouse and the underground tunnels that connect the court with the old gaol are no longer used.

② **With your back to the Supreme Court, turn left and continue up Oxford Street.** The street began as South Head Road in 1803 to access Watsons Bay Pilot Station. Now it's the home of gay pride at its proudest. The internationally famous Sydney Gay and Lesbian Mardi Gras parade draws half a million spectators to Oxford Street every year. Lower Paddington, from this point down to the city, is known as the gay precinct. Our walk is in the opposite direction, towards Paddington's historic area..

③ **Underneath the bitumen intersection of Oxford Street and Barcom Avenue lies Busby's Bore.** This water line runs from Centennial Park's swamps to the city. From 1825 to 1886 it supplied Sydney with its water after the Tank Stream became foul because of the city's overpopulation.

④ **On the corner of Greens Road and Oxford Street** were the Turnpike Tolls where South Head Road users had to stop to pay their toll from 1848 to 1877. Just up the street outside the walls of Victoria Barracks you can see the Busby Bore pump, where from 1868 locals would collect their water.

⑤ **Turn left into Glenmore Road and Paddington Village.** This tightly packed cluster of shops sprouted in 1840 when merchants settled here to do business with the workers employed to build the nearby barracks, which we'll discover a little later. Until then, much of the area was used to graze dairy cows. Cross over Glenmore Road to the corner of Gipps Street to the oldest pub in Paddington. Established in 1850, and rebuilt in 1890, The Rose and Crown Hotel has only recently had its name changed.

⑥ **Continue along Glenmore Road.** This road was cut by bullocks lugging gin from the Glenmore Distillery at Frog Hollow (now Trumper Park) to

Oxford Street. The beasts found the most level path up the hill and created a bumpy track that crossed over several creeks. Land grants on either side of Glenmore Road formed a belt of now demolished magnificent houses on grand estates. Nos. 61–63 and 95 Glenmore Road are good examples of the late 19th century sandstone terraces that followed the mansions.

> *The Glenmore Distillery was built by three partners, Robert Cooper, James Underwood and Frances Forbes, on a 40.5 hectare lower Paddington grant at the bottom of Elizabeth Street. When the men differed, Underwood bought his partners out and in 1839 subdivided some of his land and called it Paddington.*

(7) **Turn right into Liverpool Street to view the fine rows of terraces.** Elaborate decorations line the facades of the houses. Much of Paddington's filigree iron lace work was initially imported, but as construction grew so too did Sydney-based industries of supply. Ultimately, English-inspired lace work was replaced by Australiana designs, such as fishbone ferns, wattles and waratahs. Typically, the walls are stuccoed and plaster moulded with an Italianate or Classical design.

(8) **Turn right again into Spring Street, pass the tiny playground, then turn left into Prospect Street and left again into Gipps Street.** You're now in the original Paddington Village, where English, Irish and Scottish stonemasons, quarrymen, carpenters and convicts built their own houses while they constructed Victoria Barracks. Their homes were mainly of two types: the three-roomed weatherboard single storey and the four-roomed two storey. Only 25 per cent of these labourers owned their homes; almost everyone rented from absentee landlords. Gipps, Prospect and Shadforth are the oldest streets in Paddington.

(9) **Turn right into Shadforth Street** where you have a great view of Victoria Barracks. Designed by Lieutenant Colonel George Barney, the barracks were built with sandstone quarried at the site. It took convict gangs seven years to conquer the foundation's shifting sand dunes. In 1848, about 700 soldiers and officers finally moved in. Until then the military lived at George Street's Wynyard Barracks. The men complained bitterly about the move. Paddington was too far from the pubs and the sand caused havoc with eye disease. Also, several soldiers lost their children when sand hills collapsed on them while they played. The sand was ultimately used to fill Rushcutters Bay and Woolloomooloo.

(10) **Turn left into Oxford Street and continue up the left-hand side of the road** past the

old Royal Hospital for Women site. The Benevolent Society was Australia's first charity and they established this hospital in 1820. It has now been transferred to Randwick, but two of the site's original 1902 buildings have been retained, the rest bulldozed.

⑪ **Continue to the corner of Oatley Road** to see Paddington Town Hall, now a cinema, theatre and library. The first Paddington Council meetings were held in 'buxom' Jane Beard's Paddington Inn up the road. She lost her husband after only a few years of marriage and managed the pub on her own. When this building was finished in 1891 Paddingtonians finally had their own town hall. At the time it was Sydney's most affluent suburb, second only to Balmain.

⑫ **Pass the 1885 Post Office on your left, and stand on the corner of Ormond and Oxford streets,** with Juniper Hall in front of you. For many years this house was the biggest in the district. It belonged to Robert Cooper, his wife and the 28 children they shared. Cooper was a well-liked Sydney identity, sent here in 1812 for smuggling French wines and silks into Britain. After the death of his first two wives, he promised his third wife the finest home in the colony and in 1824 built Juniper Hall. Cooper co-owned the Glenmore Gin Distillery and the house was named after the gin ingredient, the juniper berry.

⑬ **Turn left into Ormond Street,** and head for what remains of one of Paddington's grand villas — Engehurst. Between Nos. 56a and 56b is a fragment of the 1830s Georgian mansion designed by John Verge for the Hely family, who owned this estate until 1868. Engehurst had about 16 huge rooms, a flagged verandah, with 10 feet long front doors that faced Glenmore Road. The Hely family sold Engehurst to John Elly Begg.

(14) **By turning right into Olive Street, then left into Heeley Street,** you'll find the remains of Olive Bank Villa to your left, now part of a childrens' day care centre. When Engehurst was bought by the Begg family, it was clear they were slowly gathering one of the area's most impressive property portfolios. In 1869 the Beggs rented Engehurst out and began to build another splendid home — Olive Bank Villa. When complete, Olive Bank took up almost half of the original Engehurst estate. Its entrance hall alone was 9 feet wide and 60 feet long. Around this time J.E. Begg Jnr bought Juniper Hall (then known as Ormond Hall), adding a third home to the family's list.

John Elly Begg was one of the 'merchant princes' that became wealthy by providing colonials with their essentials, and sometimes luxury goods. His son, John Elly Begg Jnr, made his money from the Glenmore Gin Distillery, which he part-owned.

(15) **Go down Heeley Street to Glenmore Road and Five Ways.** The corner shop provided Paddington's social life, information and communication. By 1890 there was one family grocery store for every 45 houses. If there wasn't a shop on the corner there was a pub. The Royal Hotel was built in 1888 and is the only Paddington hotel with cast-iron lace balconies.

(16) **Continue down Glenmore Road to the beginning of Gurner Street,** marked by the Anglican Church of St George, built in 1890 on land that was originally part of John Gurner's grant when just under half of Paddington's population was Anglican, a quarter Roman Catholic and one-twelfth Presbyterian.

(17) **Cascade Street** was a charming waterfall that tumbled down rocks here. Called Glenmore Falls, it was dammed to feed the Glenmore Gin Distillery below, and again for the construction of Glenmore Road. The dips in the road show you where the waterfall cascaded.

(18) **Walk up Cascade Street and turn left into Paddington Street,** which is lined with classical two-storey terraces. Many of the 1880s' boom buyers were builders, who would live in one terrace while constructing another next door. And so they would move on down their allotments, living in and renting out their

Around 1863 this sloping valley was known as Rushcutters Valley. Chinese market gardens grew down towards the bay. They were abandoned in 1910 because of racist opposition. The land was reclaimed to build the White City tennis courts. When the mad flurry of subdivision started, the grand houses were destroyed. In 1873 there were 864 houses in Paddington — 10 years later there were 2347.

completed terraces, and then moving on to the next.

(19) Turn right into Elizabeth Street, to the single-storey workers' cottages at Nos. 55 and 57. The two-storey terraces from No. 35 down were added later to fill in the vacant land.

(20) By turning right into Underwood Street you're entering one of the first areas in Paddington to be subdivided. This is part of the James Underwood 40.5 hectare grant that he sold off in 1839. Underwood, who arrived in chains with the First Fleet and returned to England a wealthy man, was the only convict from the First Fleet to do so. Just past the 1875 London Tavern you'll see a row of original single-storey sandstone terraces, built in the 1840s for soldiers' families. By 1860, this was one of the most important residential addresses in Paddington.

(21) Continue up Underwood Street to Oxford Street where, if it's a Saturday, you can visit Paddington Markets. Catch the 380 or 382 bus here back to Circular Quay.

During the Great Depression many people could not pay their rents. They were evicted from the terraces and many houses became derelict and were vandalised. By the end of the Second World War there were plans to knock down much of the suburb, straighten out the streets and build high-rise apartment blocks. In the early 1950s, however, Mediterranean migrants began to buy the affordable homes and Paddington was saved.

WALK 20

CENTENNIAL PARK

START POINT:	Paddington Gates on the corner of Oxford Street and Lang Road.
FINISH:	Paddington Gates.
HOW TO GET THERE:	Catch the 380 or 382 bus from Circular Quay up Oxford Street and get off at the corner of Queen Street.
LENGTH:	About 4 kilometres.
WALKING TIME:	1.5 hours.
ACTUAL TIME:	Anything up to 3 hours.
RATING:	Easy: most of the walk is on grass, with no hills.
WEATHER CHECK:	In the event of a downpour there are two shelters for protection.
REFRESHMENTS:	Only one cafe and kiosk open. Picnic lunch highly recommended.

The park is suitable for wheelchairs and strollers.

a tranquil oasis 5 kilometres from the city, this park has a grand Victorian feeling to its sweeping greens and grasslands with landscaped ponds surrounded by native trees and birdlife. A lazy network of leisure roads and pathways leads you through pine groves, English rose gardens and artificial lakes. This romantic parkland could not be further from Centennial Park's original landscape. It was a low-lying swampy, sandy wasteland with a healthy kangaroo population. Sydney's first settlers realised the land had a special significance in the early 1800s, when precious water flowed abundantly from its swamps. They called the area the Lachlan Swamps, and from 1825 to 1886 it supplied Sydney with drinking water. A 3.6 kilometre tunnel called Busby's Bore was dug by convicts to connect it with Hyde Park. Civil engineer John Busby suggested the bore when the city's Tank Stream ran dry and turned foul. Now we know the park's 209 hectares are part of the Botany Basin — a huge natural drainage area. The area had earlier been set aside as the Sydney Common, where people could graze their animals rather than in private and public gardens. But by the early 1850s Lachlan Swamp's 'soft, transparent and tasteless' water had begun to run dry too. So Busby's Bore was cut off in 1887. Fresh from England where elegant city parks were all the rage, Lord Carrington, New South Wales' new governor, expressed concern that Sydneysiders had nowhere to 'ride and drive'. The vision was born and Centennial Park has grown into one of Australia's loveliest inner-city havens.

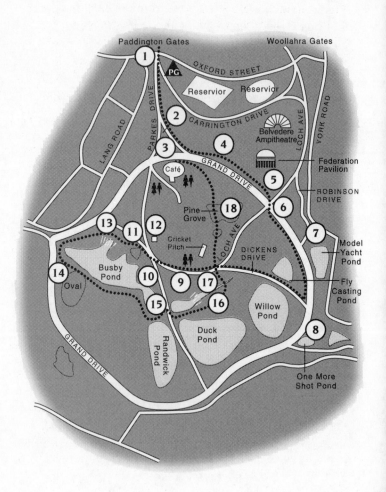

POINTS OF INTEREST ALONG THE WAY

(1) Start your walk at the sandstone Paddington Gates on the corner of Oxford Street and Lang Road. As you cross the old cobblestones, notice the lamps on top of the gates — built for gas, but now electric. The gates were built in 1887. On your left is the 1891 James Barnet-designed Park Superintendent's house. **Take the road on the right.**

(2) The Sir Henry Parkes statue divides the road in two and is also the site of the park's dedication ceremony. New South Wales' premier, Sir Henry was a charismatic politician who championed the idea of building a park to celebrate 100 years of European settlement. On 26 January 1888, Australia Day, 40,000 people watched visiting state governors sign documents that signalled the park's birth. **Take the road to your left.**

(3) You'll soon pass a Tommaso Sani statue of an 1893 rugby player, with cannon by his side. This is one of more than 40 statues that used to decorate the park. Now there are only about five. The rest were knocked down by people learning to drive cars, or blown up by university students on muck-up days.

(4) The Grand Parade was one of the park's first structures to be completed. About 150 labourers cut this road out of rock and scrub. A further 435 men, employed through a 19th century work relief program, moved sandhills and filled trenches. Now there are 22 kilometres of roads and pathways, with 67 staff overseeing the park's care. That number includes 7 horticulturists to tend the gardens, 2 arborists to look after the trees, and another 13 workers to manage the turf and waste.

(5) Keep walking to your left until you pass Federation Valley, with the sandstone Federation Pavilion. Designed by competition winner Alexander Tzannes, the pavilion houses the 1901 Commonwealth Stone. This hexagonal granite stone was placed under the table used by Queen Victoria when she signed the Act that made Australia a federation of six states. There are big celebrations planned for this valley for the 2001 centenary of Federation.

(6) The majority of the trees along the Grand Drive are Port Jackson figs, Holm oaks and Norfolk Island pines. There are also some Moreton Bay fig trees. The main difference between the figs is their size. The Moreton Bay figs are bigger, broader and have larger leaves than the Port Jackson figs.

Charles Moore was the director of the Botanic Gardens until 1896. He was replaced by Joseph Maiden, who preferred native plants to Moore's exotic foreign species. In Maiden's first year 280 trees, such as Norfolk Island pines, paperbarks, Port Jackson and Moreton Bay figs, were planted. The following year a further 200 native trees were planted. Of the park's first 11,000 trees, half died. Moore knew the indigenous species would thrive.

(7) **Pass Loch Avenue** until you have the Model Yacht Pond on your left and the Fly Casting Pond on your right. When fishing in the park was legal, people used to practise casting here.

Only 5 millimetres of rain is enough to move tonnes of litter from surrounding stormwater drains into these ponds. They are natural holding dams for stormwater run-off. A 20 millimetre downpour will flush the pollution several kilometres south into Botany Bay.

(8) **Stand and look left down towards** the One More Shot and Musgrave ponds, where lake cleaners once found hundreds of neatly wrapped parcels of dog poo. Somebody may have thought they were doing the right thing by pooper-scooping their dog's excrement and disposing of it. But the plastic bags ended up here to cause a massive pond fill.

(9) **Turn right at the next road, Dickens Drive, and follow it until you come to the Avenue of Palms.** In 1908, in search of a tree that would flourish in Sydney, 270 Canary Island palms were planted here in an experiment. They grew well, until a wilting disease attacked them and others to the north and south of Sydney. Over the last seven years 300 of the park's palms have been replaced with a cotton palm species, but horticulturists have discovered this species has contracted the disease too.

10 Notice the statue on top of a tall column soon to your left. The column used to grace the front of Sydney's old Australian Museum in William Street. The statue was positioned in 1890 and was manufactured by Luxembourg company Villeroy and Bosch. It has a sister column coming up soon.

In 1888, the park's planners were fighting infertile, sour soil, sand and an unidentified plant disease, all of which proved extremely difficult to establish plants. Not even the grass would grow. Much of this area was surrounded by windbreak fences to protect the grass seedlings, which died anyway and were replanted.

11 **Cross Parkes Drive and walk past the Rose Garden on your left.** This pretty collection of flowerbeds began in 1909. They're planted in a French parterre — rounded flowerbeds. On one Sunday in 1917, nearly 20,000 people came to see the 'Rosarium's' blooms.

(12) The Bird Sanctuary is further up Parkes Drive, but it's closed for regeneration. There are usually about 100 mostly native bird species in the sanctuary that come and go — the long grass simulates their natural habitat.

(13) **On your left you'll soon spot a sandstone bridge; cross it and leave the road to walk around the right side of Busby's Pond.** John Busby's bore starts near the Robertson Park Road entrance that you can see near the drainage corner of this pond. When it flowed freely it supplied Sydney with 2 million litres of water a day.

(14) **Continue around the pond to the path immediately on**

your left that is lined with queen and phoenix palms. Convicts built this footway. Native paper-bark trees thrive along waterways and were planted along these banks to protect the more vulnerable plants on the pond's nesting islands. **On your right is the McKay Sports Ground and the Mission Fields.**

(15) **Soon you'll come to the 1898 shelter pavilion, built between Busby's and Randwick ponds.** Sadly, all of Centennial Park's ponds are sick. This whole area holds the stormwater run-off from Randwick, Waverley, Kensington and Paddington. The run-off in the ponds is a mixture of blue-green and red algae, sediment and litter. In plain English,

the pond water has become toxic. A pond restoration program is under way to improve the water quality with some of the park's 12 ponds being dredged. Natural oil and pollution filters such as reeds and rushes are being established in others.

(16) Walk behind the pavilion and across Parkes Drive (the Avenue of Palms), where the Lily Pond is on the left and Duck Pond on the right. Between these ponds was one of the most difficult jumps in the cross-country horseracing event that was held here for decades. The event was cancelled for environmental reasons.

(17) Pass the white wooden bridge on the left and continue through the wooded area known as Lachlan Swamp. The original swamp was 3.6 kilometres in length with a catchment area of up to 600 hectares. It's known this area was well used by a small Aboriginal sub-tribe. Some say middens of seafood shells were found in the bush beyond the learners' cycleway. Well-worn Aboriginal pathways were recorded between Port Jackson (Sydney Harbour) and further south to Botany Bay and Port Hacking.

(18) Cross Dickens Drive, go over the cricket pitch and into the Pine Grove, where your nose is tickled with the fresh smell of pines. Cross the open parkland, where you can see

the Park Office and cafe on your left. Continue up to the Paddington Gates to leave the way you came in. Over the years Centennial Park has become known as The People's Park. A century ago its planners wanted to 'give city dwellers exposure to nature, so as to educate the working classes in things of natural beauty and elevate the spirit'.

> As you walk towards the Paddington Gates, on the right, well beyond the Children's Playground and up the stairs, is a superb 1899 reservoir, one of Sydney's oldest. It supplies the city and the Eastern Suburbs with water.

WALK 21

BONDI BEACH TO BRONTE BEACH

START POINT:	North Bondi Beach.
FINISH:	Bronte Beach.
HOW TO GET THERE:	Catch the train to Bondi Junction where the 380 bus leaves regularly for Bondi Beach. Ask the driver to let you off at the northern end.
LENGTH:	3 kilometres.
WALKING TIME:	1 hour.
ACTUAL TIME:	At least 1 hour from Bondi to Bronte; the return trip is usually quicker.
RATING:	Some steep stone steps, but an easy concrete path.
WEATHER CHECK:	A great sunny or cloudy day walk, though there's no shelter after Bondi.
REFRESHMENTS:	There's always a cafe open at Bondi and until sunset there are cafes serving good food at Bronte.

Unsuitable for wheelchairs and strollers.

*t*his kilometre of sand represents a beach culture that has taken white Australians 200 years to perfect. Somehow Bondi manages to completely capture the Aussie's love of stripping off, hanging around in the sun and then heading off for a few beers. The beach has a million different moods, each one more beautiful than the last. Visitors often note how the Australian sky seems so big. This Bondi walk, with its huge sky, sparkling Pacific Ocean and rugged cliffs, is spectacular. The area has always been a popular family spot. Some 150 years ago white settlers would paddle along the shoreline while their horses waited in the sand dunes. But even in those days people kept taking off more clothes than was permitted. Modesty laws ensured women wore skirts over their neck-to-knee swimming costumes, and loitering on the beach was prevented by allowing only 30 minutes in the water. By the 1960s the laws were somewhat more relaxed, but still beach inspectors with tape measures pursued women in bikinis to make sure there was at least 4 inches of fabric on their hips. Nowadays scantily clad bodies from all over the world strut along the promenade. First recorded as Bundi Bay, then Boondi and Bundye, the name comes from the area's original inhabitants — the Cadigals and the Birrabirragals. In their Dharug dialect, Bondi means the sound of tumbling water. We'll direct you to their rock art and tell you more about their culture. This is an easy path that connects the cliffs with three of Sydney's most popular 'inner-city' beaches — Bondi, Tamarama and Bronte. Remember your swimmers, and take a picnic lunch.

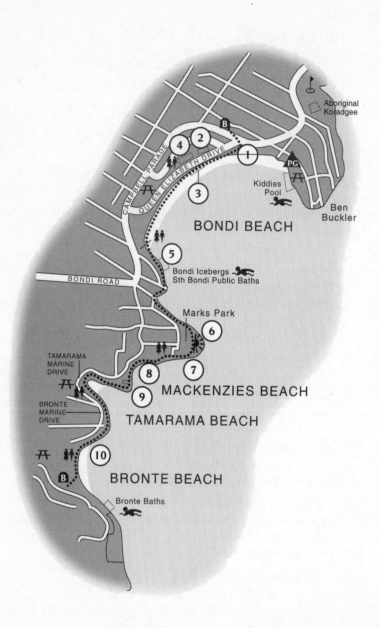

POINTS OF INTEREST ALONG THE WAY

(1) **The walk starts at the northern end of the beach's promenade. To get your bearings, walk across one of the graceful 1920s pedestrian bridges from Campbell Parade, or just cut across Bondi Park and head for the beach.** Face the sea. On your left is North Bondi, where families gather near the wading pool. The North Bondi point and cliffs are called Ben Buckler — notice the 235 tonne boulder that washed up onto the rocks during a violent storm in 1912. On your right is South Bondi, where the law has turned a blind eye to topless sunbathing since 1978.

(2) **Walk along the promenade with the North Bondi Surf**

Three of the greatest Australian beach hazards are rips, bluebottles and dumpers. Rips are dangerous currents stirred up by shifting sandbanks. Rips drag swimmers out to sea. If you're caught in one, don't panic — float with the rip, don't swim against it, and wave at the beach. Bluebottles are small blue jellyfish with long trailing tentacles that sting like mad. To relieve the sting, head for your nearest surf life saving club for vinegar, then apply a soothing lotion. Dumpers are big curling waves that dump you (usually head first) into the sand when

Life Saving Club on your right. The 256 surf life saving clubs across Australia play an essential role in surfing safety. In this century alone, they've pulled half a million drowning people from the surf. It's a volunteer job. The men are internationally famous for the way they pull their swimmers up their bottoms so they can get a grip on the slippery wooden seats of the life savers' boat. Remember, when a life saver waves at you, don't wave back. They're signalling you're in some kind of danger.

(3) After the Bondi Surf Life Saving Club, you'll notice a big brown watchtower on your left. It's called the Shark Tower, but life savers no longer watch from here, as no-one has been taken by a shark since meshing was placed around Sydney beaches in 1937. Sharks are sometimes caught in the nets — hammerheads, grey nurses, tigers and white pointers. Over the last century, 400 people in Australia have

Black Sunday: in 1938 Bondi Beach was packed with 35,000 people to see a surf carnival. Three huge freak waves smashed onto the beach and 250 people were dragged out to sea. 150 were rescued unharmed, but 60 suffered immersion, 35 were rescued unconscious and 5 people died.

been attacked by sharks, but you're 50 times more likely to drown. Attached to the tower is a Beachwatch sign, which gives current temperatures, tidal information and water pollution levels.

(4) Bondi Pavilion, and its predecessor, was built to stop people changing into their bathing costumes in the local scrub. Until 1902 it was an offence to swim in daylight. By 1912, surfing had become so popular Waverley

Council had to build changing accommodation for 1000 people. In the late 1920s this pavilion was built to cater for 12,000 people. In those days people danced the night away in a ballroom, or lazed about in Turkish baths. Now the pavilion serves as a community centre and theatre.

Turn left into Notts Avenue after the wooden stairs at the very end of the South Bondi promenade.

(5) The Bondi Icebergs Club is above South Bondi's Public Baths. More commonly referred to as 'the Bergs', the club is famous for its weird initiation rites. To get into the swing in winter, members throw blocks of ice into the water. To be a member of the club you must first swim here at least three Sundays out of four for five years, whatever the weather and with good humour. About 90 per cent of applicants don't make the grade, but 600 men (it's a men only club) maintain the vigil.

When the Sydney Eora tribe realised the Europeans had come to stay, they tried to fight back. It's said the warriors built a network of underground workshops where the pavilion and Campbell Parade now stand. Here they made their axes, spears and knives. Their armouries are buried beneath the bitumen.

(6) **After 'the Bergs', stairs lead off to your left. The coastal path begins here with the first rocky inlet, then stone stairs bring you up to a round lookout point.** The furthest southern headland you can see from here is Maroubra. Originally these cliffs backed onto sand dunes and scrub. When the first settlers came they noted and used tracks that crisscrossed and connected the dunes. The tracks were native trade routes. Studies have identified 34 Aboriginal clans in and around the Sydney area. The

In the distance at North Bondi is a golf course where a tall, disused sewerage vent is clearly visible. At its base is a koradgee, or ancient Aboriginal priest's grounds. The carvings depict a whale, fish and people. Stranded whales represented a feast and a celebration. To view them, walk towards the golf course via Campbell Parade/Military Road — but after this walk.

Cadigals and Birrabirragals here were not tall, but stocky and strong. In winter they wore long, flowing possum fur coats; in summer, only their belts and their weapons. They decorated their hair with animal teeth and lobster claws. The women carried kangaroo sinew for binding and sewing and flint stones to make fires in over-the-shoulder woven bags, as well as pieces of paperbark for holding water. In 1788 there were 60 Cadigals, but two years later there were only 3 left. They were shot, poisoned or became sick with white men's diseases.

(7) About 30 metres from the lookout on your left are Aboriginal carvings of a huge fish. The carvings were re-grooved by Waverley Council in 1962.

(8) Mackenzies Beach was originally Mackenzies Waverley Dairy. During the 1880s cows grazed in the hills behind the beach.

(9) Pause beside the Tamarama Surf Life Saving Club and imagine this tiny beach, its cliffs and the gully behind it as one big fun park. From 1887 to 1911, rides, slides and animal shows

completely enveloped this tiny cove. Firstly The Aquarium opened in 1887, then 'Wonderland City' followed in 1906. A steam-driven miniature scenic railway wrapped itself around the cliffs and across the beach on 2 miles of timber and papier-mache tracks. An enormous balloon airship ran on a steel cable from cliff to cliff. In what was known as Fletcher's Glen, thousands strolled around glass cages of exotic fish; seals and vaudeville acts performed around an open-air roller skating rink and a bowling alley; and attractions such as 'Alice, the elephant in a thousand' and 'Professor Godfrey's Dog and Monkey Circus' thrilled the amusement seekers. By 1911, however, the novelty had worn off and Wonderland City closed. The name Tamarama seems to be a bastardisation of its native name — *Gamma Gamma* — which, coincidentally, is pretty close to its nickname, Glamourama.

(10) Continue around Tamarama Marine Drive which turns into Bronte Marine Drive. Keep an eye out for the path off to the left which leads you down to Bronte Beach. During spring and summer pods of dolphins can sometimes be seen here. Whales heading north with their calves also make the odd visit. The most common fish are tailor, bream, blackfish and red morwong. The baths at the southern end of the beach were built in 1887, when men and women were not allowed to bathe together. To solve the problem, men swam in the morning and evening and women bathed during the day. It's assumed Bronte was well used by the Cadigals because a waterfall of fresh water once poured down through its sheltered gully into a lagoon. With its nickname Brontecarlo, Bronte has always been a popular family beach.

If you don't feel like walking back you can catch the 378 bus back to Bondi Junction station. If you do walk back to Bondi, catch the 380 bus from there to the station.

> You can continue your walk past Bronte through Waverley Cemetery to Coogee. Simply follow the paths and interconnecting coastal roads. The wheelchair walk picks the path up from Coogee to Lurline Bay.

WALK 22

THE WHEELCHAIR WALK

COOGEE TO LURLINE BAY

START POINT:	North Coogee has a car park with wheelchair access to the promenade, or start at Trenerry Reserve, site number 5.
FINISH:	At the end of Trenerry Reserve where you can backtrack to Coogee Beach.
LENGTH:	1 kilometre from Coogee Beach to the 525 metre Trenerry Reserve boardwalk.
WALKING & WHEELING TIME:	Entirely up to you
RATING:	The concrete is a little bumpy past the surf life saving club where there's an incline up to the reserve's green level playing field, which must be crossed to reach the boardwalk.
WEATHER CHECK:	People should only do this do this on a fine day.
REFRESHMENTS:	Good wheelchair access to a cafe with tables on the footpath across from the Coogee Surf Life Saving Club.

*t*his walk is designed for those who find walking difficult, but enjoy the outdoors. It's for older people and those who use a wheelchair, and need level paths with rails and no steps. Randwick Council has installed a 525 metre wooden boardwalk on the southern cliffs of Coogee Beach that is perfect for people with mobility disability. The less able can do the Trenerry Reserve Boardwalk by itself, while the more energetic can start 1 kilometre away on the Coogee Beach Promenade. There are no steps to negotiate on this route, though a sometimes bumpy incline connects Coogee's Promenade to the boardwalk.

The word Coogee is Aboriginal for 'stink' or 'bad smell'. There used to be a swirling patch of water off the beach that washed seaweed onshore where it dried out and stank. Before European settlement this area was a low lying series of sand dunes surrounded by thick woods. In 1800 there was a wide gully rich in wildlife and timber where Coogee Bay Road is now. From 1810 to 1830 the first white hunters, fishermen, timber cutters and campers moved in. Tracks were created from South Head Road (now Oxford Street) and by 1832 Anzac Parade and Alison Road were established routes.

Taking the sea air had always been fashionable among the holidaying early colonials, and swimming was fast becoming Australia's most popular recreational sport. The Crown Reserves of the late 1800s had already ensured the construction of 3 seawater tidal pools. One of them is among Sydney's last remaining baths for women only.

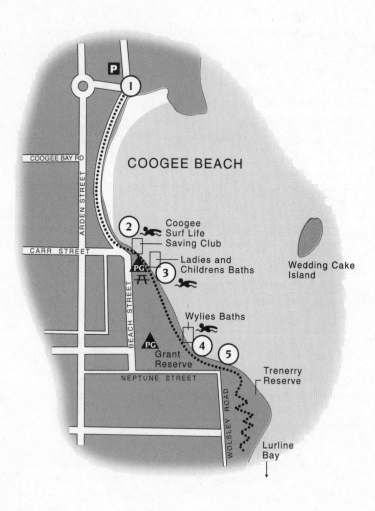

POINTS OF INTEREST ALONG THE WAY

(1) **Until 1902 swimming at Coogee Beach** was strictly segregated. Women bathed at the southern end and men at the northern end. In 1910 council tried to introduce a law that banned 'loitering clad only in a bathing costume', but the Solicitor General refused to ratify it.

(2) **Head to South Coogee and pass the Coogee Surf Life Saving Club,** which was formed in 1907. The first clubhouse dates back to 1922, the current building was constructed in 1960 and extended 12 years later. Every weekend the beach is patrolled by 14 volunteer members of the club.

The Coogee Aquarium and Swimming Baths at the northern end of the bay opened in 1887. More tourists were attracted when an amusement pier was built down the middle of the beach in 1928. It was a grand affair with a theatre seating 1400 and a ballroom for 600. A revolutionary shark-net was added in 1929. By now Coogee was firmly on the map as a seaside resort—but so were Manly, Bondi and Tamarama's Wonderland City. The competition, together with the high cost of repairs, resulted in the pier's demolition only five years later.

(3) **On your left is the Coogee Ladies' and Children's Baths, beside the Children's Playground.** This sanctuary for female bathers is between the Life Saving Club's pool and Wylie's pool. The reserve was allocated for 'women only' in 1886. One hundred years later a Coogee man challenged the 'no mixed bathing' rule with the claim it was discriminatory against men. The Ladies' Baths were granted an exemption under the Anti-Discrimination Act based on the concerns of the local Muslim women who are forbidden to bath with men present. The pool is also known as the McIver Baths — after Robert and Rose McIver who operated it from the 1920s. It is now cared for by a trust and a club.

(4) **Wylie's Baths are next door.** These baths, together with Giles Hot Sea Baths at the northern end of the beach, were reserved for public use in 1902. Wylie's remains one of Sydney's classic tidal swimming pools and is now classified by the National Trust. In 1960 the modern wooden decking and kiosk were added.

IMPORTANT NOTE: There is no wheelchair access into any of the baths at Coogee. Clovelly, the next beach north, won the 1988 National Bicentennial Access Award for the excellent

Almost 1 kilometre from land is Wedding Cake Island, so named because the seagulls regularly covered it with 'white icing' — their droppings. Apparently it was the target for army cadets practising their artillery aim in 1858. They fired 20 rounds but never managed to hit it.

wheelchair approach into Clovelly Baths.

(5) **Soon you'll come across the level green playing field of Trenerry Reserve; the boardwalk's entrance is on the other side — marked by a signpost.** Council installed the boardwalk to protect the rare wetland flora and fauna habitat underneath it. The ramp crosses wildflowers and indigenous plants native to Sydney's coastline. 37 different bird types use the area for breeding and at least 6 migratory bird species drop in for resting or

When the Coogee Beach Aquarium and Swimming Baths opened in 1887 highlights included a seal pond and an alligator pond surrounded by exotic fish tanks. During the day people would ride in the toboggan rink or sip tea in the Japanese Tea house. When the sun went down, they would watch the new 'electric picture shows', dine in the restaurant and dance to live bands. The Aquarium has been upgraded many times, but still stands on its original site.

feeding while on their way to their final destination. **The wooden ramp continues for 525 metres.**

At the time of writing, Randwick Council was negotiating with residents to continue the coastal walk in front of private properties to Maroubra

Beach. Council hopes one day
to connect all the walks from
South Head to La Perouse.

La Perouse to Henry Head and Beyond

START POINT:	La Perouse bus loop.
FINISH:	La Perouse bus loop.
HOW TO GET THERE:	The 393, 394, L94 or 398 bus from Circular Quay.
LENGTH:	9.5 kilometres.
WALKING TIME:	2.5 hours.
ACTUAL TIME:	4 to 5 hours, or a whole day.
RATING:	A moderately easy walk to the corner of Pussycat Bay, but then a rock-hop or a rough track for the fitter and more agile. You will come in contact with the bush if you stay on the high track above Pussycat Bay, so take a long-sleeved shirt for protection.
WEATHER CHECK:	Unsuitable in rain as it would be too slippery beyond Henry Head.
REFRESHMENTS:	Restaurants and cafes at La Perouse, but nothing on the rest of the walk. A picnic is recommended, and take plenty of water.

Unsuitable for wheelchairs and strollers.

*t*his walk is definitely best on Sundays. There's a wealth of monuments and historic sites to see, a fine memorabilia collection of Laperouse's expedition in the museum, the famous fort that would have crumbled under attack, and other fortifications to be climbed through and marvelled at, and the snake man with his deadly but fascinating reptiles and the boomerang throwers — a spectacle on any Sunday. To many La Perouse has the most historical significance in Australia. Even though Captain Cook actually landed at Kurnell when he first sailed into Botany Bay in 1770, it was his accurate mapping of the northern shores that led Governor Phillip and the French to La Perouse 18 years later. Cook showed running water to the west of a bare island, which today bears that name. Governor Phillip arrived on 18 January 1788 and was taking his fleet to the more sheltered anchorage at Port Jackson when the French turned up a few days later. The Aborigines had already been at La Perouse for about 7000 years and were so unimpressed by Captain Cook's arrival they didn't even bother to look up. They gave Laperouse a tough time, however, determined to drive the unwanted newcomer away. The walk meanders through bushland in the Botany Bay National Park, with Sydney red gums stretching for light. Out on the rugged coast you too can stand where 100,000 others did one May weekend over 60 years ago, to look at what's left of the unfortunate interstate collier that foundered on Cape Banks. And on the same cape stuck out over the water there's the most challenging of golf tees, where President Clinton tried his hand.

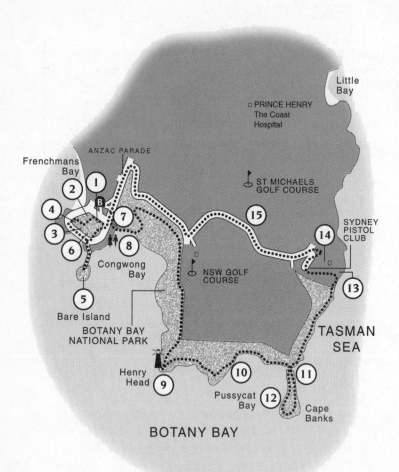

Little
Bay

□ PRINCE HENRY
The Coast
Hospital

Frenchmans
Bay

ANZAC PARADE

⛳ ST MICHAELS
GOLF COURSE

② ①

Ⓑ

④ ⑦

③ ⑧

⑥ Ⓦ

Congwong
Bay

⑤

Bare Island

BOTANY BAY
NATIONAL PARK

Henry
Head

⑨

⑮

⛳ NSW GOLF
COURSE

SYDNEY
PISTOL
CLUB

⑭

⑬

TASMAN
SEA

⑩ ⑪

Pussycat
Bay

⑫

Cape
Banks

BOTANY BAY

POINTS OF INTEREST ALONG THE WAY

(1) Leave the bus stop and head towards the large red building in the middle of the Anzac Parade loop. But first you will come to a plaque in memory of Marjorie Timbery, one of the tireless workers of the Aboriginal community. Marjorie was related by marriage to Queen Emma Timbery, one of the more colourful local characters, who was granted the land along La Perouse beach. Now there's a new feud going on among the Aborigines themselves over native title. A group calling themselves the Korewal people, who have married into the Timbery family, have made a claim for most of La Perouse's foreshore and hinterland. It's actually unclear which Aboriginal clan

> Over towards the reserve you can see the tops of three Moreton Bay figs called 'Dreaming Trees'. The one standing alone was where the old people sat and the children played, and where local identity King Billy lived in his red-painted corrugated-iron shack. This tree was dedicated to Queen Emma Timbery in 1986 by Marjorie Timbery.

lived at La Perouse when the British arrived. There's an account of some 300 Aborigines having gathered at Long Bay in June 1788 during Governor Phillip's investigation of the killing of two rushcutters. Long Bay was probably the Cadigal clan's region, but the 49 canoes pulled up on nearby Congwong Beach probably belonged to the Bidigals from around Castle Hill and the Gweagals from the south side of Botany Bay. Pemulwuy, the Aboriginal guerilla leader from the Bidigal clan, is known to have waged war from the George's River entrance to Botany Bay and west to Parramatta.

> In 1880 there were 26 Aborigines living in the 'blacks' camp' above Frenchman's Bay. The Europeans believed they were a doomed race, and mixing black and white was undesirable. The mission was moved to higher ground when the sand foundations sank. Corrugated iron was replaced with fibro and timber, but there were no bathrooms — just a pump with a hose in a bucket for a shower. The mission managers could walk in at any time for an inspection. If they thought the children weren't being looked after properly, they would just take them away, never to be seen again.

(2) Just a little further down the hill is the grave of Pere Receveur, a Franciscan friar and scientist who came to Australia aboard the *Astrolabe* and died here three weeks after the exhausted, bruised and battered French expedition limped into

Frenchman's Bay. Receveur was injured when a landing party was attacked by natives in Samoa two months earlier. Receveur's epitaph was carved in a nearby tree, sent to Paris, and now stands in a museum here.

③ **Walk on to the Laperouse Museum, open Wednesday to Sunday from 10 am to 4.30 pm.** The museum was established by a group of Australian and French residents in part of the old Cable Station building. It contains a large collection of memorabilia from the La Perouse expedition, and is well worth a look. The building itself was opened in 1882 to house staff and equipment of the cable company that laid the first ocean telegraph cable between La Perouse and Nelson in New Zealand. It was part of a worldwide link, sending and receiving international telegrams, at an initial cost of 9 shillings for every 10 words.

④ **With the museum behind you, up the path to your left is the La Perouse Monument, the tall column crowned with an astrolabe.** It was a strange quirk of history that the French arrived the very same day the British were weighing anchor to sail north to the calm waters of Port Jackson. Governor Phillip had in fact left, and it was Captain Hunter, Commander of HMS *Sirius*, who spotted the *Astrolabe* and *Boussole* outside Botany Bay. He put an officer aboard to help them land, then set sail himself

The French Colours sighted at sea by the English would have been a white flag as the present-day tricolour was not hoisted until one year later during the French Revolution. The British flag was also not as we know it, as it was missing the diagonal red cross of St Patrick which was added in 1801 to complete the Union Jack.

with his ten member fleet. Laperouse built a stockade to keep out the 'fierce' natives and the convicts wanting a lift home, and spent six weeks building new longboats and resuscitating his crew. The French and the British visited each other's camps often — Laperouse giving them journals and charts to take home. Just as well, as when the French sailed from Botany Bay on 11 March 1788, they were never seen again. The mystery of their disappearance wasn't unravelled for almost 40 years, when the remains of their ships were found wrecked at Vanikoro in the Solomon Islands. The monument to Laperouse and his brave adventurers was built and paid for by another famous French sailor, Baron de Bougainville.

⑤ **Up the road is Bare Island, which can be visited on Saturdays and Sundays for a small fee at 12.45, 1.30, 2.30 and 3.30 pm. Just wait at the gate for the guide.** When the last British troops were withdrawn from New South Wales in 1870, it was decided Bare Island should be fortified — being

Sydney's back door, Botany Bay was vulnerable to attack. The fort was finished in 1885, with five gun emplacements linked by bomb-proof passages. But the fort wasn't without controversy. The concrete was too thin — the soldiers would have been safer outside under attack than in, the guns didn't recoil and there were no foundations. During the Newcastle earthquake two of the walls fell down. The fort was turned into a war veterans' home in 1912 and the magazine rooms were converted into bedrooms, but during the world wars the veterans had to move out to make way for soldiers once again watching for invaders. The guns were sold for scrap, but were left to rust by the gate, being too heavy to cross the wooden bridge. The last time the 12 ton Armstrong cannon was fired it split down the middle and shattered many window panes in La Perouse. This gun, however, has had a $20,000 restoration, and proudly stands in its old spot, pointing out to sea. The biggest cannon, the 18 ton Armstrong, is also still there. It did go missing for a while, however — the war veterans had buried it under their snooker room! The National Parks and Wildlife Service runs the tours, and there's also a lantern light tour. Phone 0311 3379 for details.

⑥ **Back on the Scenic Drive on top of the hill is the Macquarie Watchtower,** which was built in the 1820s to house soldiers watching for enemies arriving by water. In 1831 the soldiers were replaced by customs officers in the belief that smuggling was a bigger threat than invasion. In 1868 the first school opened offering education to Europeans, local Aboriginal children, fishermen, gardeners and customs officers. The tower and surrounding buildings were dam-

---

For one member of the First Fleet, this was his second visit to Botany Bay. Peter Hibbs, at the tender age of 14 was on board Captain Cook's Endeavour when he landed at Kurnell in 1770. And he returned on HMS Sirius 18 years later. Hibbs stayed in Australia and accompanied explorer Matthew Flinders on some of his journeys.

aged by fire in 1957. The tower is now ranked as one of the oldest colonial structures in Australia.

(7) **Continue up the road to the snake pit, the colourful enclosure opposite the bus loop,** where snake men have been charming visitors for the past 100 years. The first entertainer, self-named 'Professor' Fred Fox, described himself as 'half snake juice, half English' because of the number of times he'd been bitten. As well as being a huge drawcard for La Perouse, Fox was determined to get recognition for his antidote. When ignored by the New South Wales government, Fox took his snake bite cure to India, where he died of a krait bite, which he failed to detect. George Cann reigned at the loop

The gully behind the snake pit in George Cann's time was a popular venue for two-up. But it was also a favourite haunt of the gaming squad. A raid one particular day sent punters fleeing. One fugitive was so anxious to escape he jumped over George's back fence right into his snake pen. With a blood-curdling scream and probably without his feet so much as touching the ground, the punter leapt right back out again. During the Great Depression George was known to give the terrified Chinese market gardeners a free 'charming'. With just a hint of a snake he would always be given a bag full of vegetables.

for the next 40 years, gathering his performers from the local bush. The snake man still performs on Sundays. Aboriginal craft has long been a feature of La Perouse, and the locals will still throw a boomerang or sell you one, if you come by on Sundays.

(8) **This is your last chance to visit the toilets before heading bush. Go down the steps to Congwong Beach, walk across and stay on this side of the fence. Walk up the sandy, then concrete road, but don't go straight ahead up the fenced path — it leads to an unofficial nude beach.** There were a number of Aboriginal middens, leftovers from centuries of seafood feasting, but some were destroyed when sand was taken from the back of Congwong Beach to build the extension to the north-south runway at Sydney Airport. During the Great Depression hundreds of people set up home here in an unemployment camp known as Happy Valley. Conditions in the camp were appalling. Many squatters had no bedclothes, the wind cut through their tents which were infested with fleas, flies and mosquitoes, there was no running water and food was scarce. But everyone helped where they could. Local fishermen gave them salmon; the Chinese market gardeners donated vegetables; dairy farmers handed out milk; and the golf course piped in water. When the Depression ended many

> *As the adults had trouble making ends meet after the Depression, the Aboriginal children were 'making hay'. They could make up to 10 pounds a day, diving for tourists' coins tossed off the wharf. They also sold golf balls and local flowers, but a more palatable pastime was collecting five-corner berries.*

squatters refused to leave, preferring the dole.

About 100 metres before you hit the main road, turn right at the arrow and head off along the bush track. The Botany Bay National Park has more than 350 different sorts of plants. Many of the species recorded by Banks and Solander during Captain Cook's visit more than 200 years ago can still be seen. In this exposed area the heathland bush is dense and low with scrubby tea-trees, banksias and acacias.

Keep on the main path, turn right at the various arrows, and follow the Henry Head signs. Up on the ridge look back towards Port Botany and Yarra Bay. Millions of dollars have been spent turning Botany Bay into a viable shipping operation, after Governor Phillip moved on claiming the bay too shallow even for his diminutive First Fleet. Banks Wall, a 1.5 kilometre man-made breakwater, curves its way into the bay, providing anchorage for container and bulk liquid ships. And behind that is the ANL terminal.

⑨ When you reach the sealed road turn right towards the sea and Henry Head. The fortifications on the headland were ready for action ten years after Bare Island. They contained two 6 inch breech-loading disappearing guns which could fire across the bay, searchlights, barracks and observation posts. Don't miss the disappearing gun pit on the western side of the lighthouse — it's huge. The gun would pop up, fire, and hopefully retract without a 'whiff' of smoke, so the enemy couldn't tell where the shot had come from. On Bare Island their gun wouldn't come down, and left a huge cloud of black smoke, leaving an telltale target for the enemy. During the Great Depression the Henry Head fortifications were used by the unemployed as squats. The headland is a palette of colour in the spring, with a stunning display of native wildflowers.

Stay on the same level as the easternmost gun emplacement (not the highest lookout) and head towards the ocean on the rock ledge, which turns into a path, and leads down to a ledge on the cliff top.

⑩ Continue to the point of Pussycat Bay where you can see the golf course on your left, the sea below and the wreck directly ahead. The *Minmi*, on its way from Melbourne to Newcastle, thought it was 4.5 kilometres offshore when it ploughed into Cape Banks at full speed in a peasoup fog in May 1937. The pounding sea broke the ship in two, separating the 24 seamen on board. Members of the artillery garrison were woken by the sound of escaping steam, and were astounded to see the Minmi on the rocks. They secured a rope over 30 metres of seething white water, and six men winched themselves hand over foot to land. One man died in the boiling sea. The others were brought ashore the next day in calmer conditions — the cook died on board when the ship split in two.

Now you either retrace your steps, or if you're fit and agile keep going. Make an educated decision on whether to stay on the narrow top track (where the bush is close at times) or go down to your right and onto the flat rocks below — but check the tide first. If waves are breaking onto the shelf, stay high. You will notice signs on the rocks warning not to take the shellfish or seafood. These species are protected and it is illegal to take them.

The paths converge on the sandy beach up to your left, by the cave. Continue on the rocks or above the waterline on the rough track until you reach the bridge crossing onto Cape Banks.

(11) Just over the bridge is the Championship Tee of the par 36th hole of the New South Wales Golf Course. This pic-

The Coast had its own leper colony — a permanent population of 30 to 40 people. Because of the contagious nature of the disease they were inmates for life, but filled in their days caring for the huge 202 hectare hospital grounds. One leper held the position of head gardener for 21 years, despite being fingerless on one hand. The Coast was also popular with itinerant 'bob-a-day' men, as they were paid double for danger money.

turesque 177 metre hole over the water can test the ability of any golfer hitting into a strong westerly. US President Bill Clinton landed just short when he hit off from here in November 1996. His playing partner, the Shark — Greg Norman — made the green.

(12) **Walk down to inspect the wreck which has now been pushed round into Pussycat Bay,** as 100,000 others did on the May weekend the Minmi foundered. The road from La Perouse was closed, leaving sightseers a 3 kilometre trek. Dozens of police were called in to supervise the crowd and golf was abandoned for the day because of the crush.

Recross the bridge, and head up the right-hand side of the golf course on the wide sandy path. Stay left when you have a chance to go right, and at the top of the hill you will come out on a grassy oval, which leads onto a road.

(13) **You have reached the Cape Banks fortifications,** which became the main coastal defence system for the area in the Second World War, superseding Henry Head. This much larger establishment was armed by two 9.2 inch guns that could fire 26,400 metres and a battery of anti-aircraft guns. It also contained plotting rooms, torpedo launching facilities, barracks, a hospital and its own electricity generating plant. The big guns were on the eastern ridge and the southern hilltop, behind the path you came up on. Incidentally, none of these guns was ever fired in anger, but lots of practice went on.

(14) **Follow the sealed road past the pistol range on your right and in a few minutes you will see the headstones at the Coast Hospital cemetery. Wander through and read the headstones.** Most of these people died of infectious diseases in the early years of the Coast Hospital, now called Prince Henry, the establishment on the skyline. The hospital began as a refuge for smallpox victims in

1881, when this deadly, disfiguring disease reached epidemic proportions and victims were housed in tents in an isolation camp on the beach. After this outbreak, the 'Coast' expanded and became Sydney's infectious diseases hospital, treating the plague, Spanish flu brought home by First World War military personnel, in fact any infectious disease except venereal disease in women, which wasn't recognised by the government even though it was rife.

(15) **Continue along the narrow road, watching and listening for traffic.** The golf course on your right is St Michael's, named after Michael Moran, 'to give himself a lift' as he put it. The original land was leased from Moran. **Turn right at the stop sign at the entrance to the New South Wales Golf Course. If you want to take a short cut back to Congwong Beach look for the barricade to the track on the left, which says 'No Parking', or stay on the road to the Anzac Parade intersection. There you turn left back to the bus stop, to catch the bus back to Circular Quay.**

> *North of the hospital the Aborigines too had their own infectious diseases ward, known as the Blacks' Hospital. On the south side of Long Bay, known as Boora, there's a large rock overhang where Aborigines suffering smallpox and other diseases gathered, and mostly died, as they had no immunity.*

WALK 24

KURNELL TO CAPE BAILY

START POINT:	Captain Cook Drive at Kurnell — the Monument Track, Captain Cook's Landing Place.
FINISH:	The Discovery Centre, Captain Cook's Landing Place.
HOW TO GET THERE:	By train from Town Hall or Central to Cronulla station, then catch the Cronulla bus to Kurnell.
LENGTH:	9.5 kilometres.
WALKING TIME:	3 hours.
ACTUAL TIME:	4 to 6 hours.
RATING:	This is a moderately strenuous long walk which includes a short, sandy climb to the lighthouse.
WEATHER CHECK:	The Cape Solander to Cape Baily section would be miserable and hazardous in the rain.
REFRESHMENTS:	There are two takeaway shops near the bus stop and a coin-operated drink machine outside the Discovery Centre, so take a picnic and plenty of water.

Suitable for wheelchairs and strollers around the Monument Track only.

*g*rassy, sleepy, isolated Kurnell has more historical significance than any other place in Australia. This is where the nation was born. Lieutenant James Cook and the crew of the *Endeavour* set foot on Australian soil here on 29 April 1770. The lieutenant — he wasn't made a captain until he returned home — spent eight days charting the bay and recording the peculiar plants and animals. Cook initially called the bay Stingray Bay because of their prevalence here, but changed it to Botanists Bay, which was too clumsy, so it became Botany Bay. On this walk you pass through manicured parkland and see the landmarks honouring the early explorers. It wasn't only Cook who put Kurnell on the map — so did the Caltex (now Ampol) Oil Refinery, with its contortion of pipes and tanks filling the skyline. Caltex not only brought to Kurnell the biggest oil-refining operation in Australia, but also contact with the outside world. Part of the deal was to link the remote fishing village to Cronulla by road. Out on the coast there's a dramatic change of scene as the ocean pounds the majestic sandstone cliffs, forging spectacular deep ravines. The unique heathland comes to life in summer in a blaze of colour, attracting a wide variety of honey- and seed-eating birds. You might also catch a glimpse of the rare peregrine falcon, an albatross sheltering from a storm, or the beautiful white-crested sea eagle. The famous Kurnell sandhills were the sets of many box-office hits, including 40,000 *Horsemen* and *Mad Max*, but now most of the dunes are gone, to become the sand in the cement of Sydney's building trade.

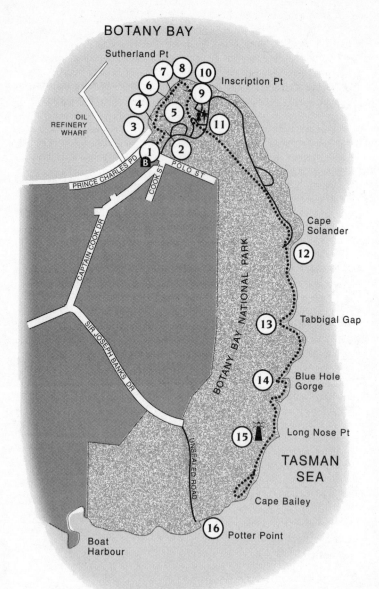

BOTANY BAY

Sutherland Pt

7 8 10

6

Inscription Pt

4 9

OIL
REFINERY
WHARF

5

3 11

1
B 2

PRINCE CHARLES PD POLO ST

COOK ST

CAPTAIN COOK DR

Cape
Solander

12

SIR JOSEPH BANKS DR

BOTANY BAY NATIONAL PARK

13 Tabbigal Gap

14 Blue Hole
Gorge

15 Long Nose Pt

TASMAN
SEA

UNSEALED ROAD

Cape Bailey

Boat
Harbour

16 Potter Point

POINTS OF INTEREST
ALONG THE WAY

(1) Walk into the park on the sealed Monument Track and head towards the water. Thousands of years ago Botany Bay didn't look anything like it does today. The Kurnell peninsula was an island separated by the Cooks and the Georges rivers just north of Cronulla. **The plaque on your right** shows where Captain Cook's landing party allegedly sank their first well.

(2) On your right is Cook's Obelisk, paid for and erected by Thomas Holt in April of the first centenary year, after the anniversary went past without official recognition. It wasn't until 1899 that 100 hectares of land were set aside as public park in recognition of Cook and his crew and the local Dharawal-speaking

Gweagal Aboriginal clan. Cook's first meeting with the locals was hostile. There are various interpretations as to who were the aggressors, but spears were thrown and one Aborigine was hit with musket shot. The Gweagal clan glued their hair in thrums, making it look like a mop.

(3) Directly to your left out on the rocks is a plaque marking where Cook came ashore.

(4) Further along is the remains of the ferry shelter, and out into the water beside the row of trees is all that's left of the wharf. The ferry from La Perouse was the chief form of transport to Kurnell before the opening of Captain Cook Drive in 1953. The ferry service was discontinued in 1957. It reopened briefly eight years later, but wasn't patronised. Kurnell residents are trying to have the La Perouse ferry restarted, as a trade-off for the increased air traffic from the opening of the third runway at Mascot.

(5) The next monument honours Sir Joseph Banks, a wealthy young Englishman and Oxford scholar who paid for his own botanical party on the *Endeavour*.

(6) The stream on your right is where Cook's party found water. Accompanying Governor Phillip, a First Fleet party cleared

It's believed about 200 Aboriginal people from the Kurnell-Cronulla district were on their way to a corroboree with Illawarra groups when they were caught in a violent thunderstorm crossing the Hacking River at Little Turriell Point. They sheltered under an overhang which collapsed when it was struck by lightning, killing everybody. The mouth of the cave was blasted open in 1918, uncovering a large number of bones and artefacts. This might explain why there were so few natives at Kurnell when Cook arrived 30 to 40 years later.

this stream in January 1788, just in case Port Jackson proved unsuitable for settlement.

(7) The first land grant of 283 hectares was made to merchant James Birnie, who built a small stone cottage on the hill for his foreman and convict labourers. The semi-literate convict clerk entered the name 'Half-a-Farm' in the Register of Land Grants. Alpha Farm was the real name, being Greek for 'first'. But being all Greek to the convict, he wrote it phonetically.

> *Kurnell's 'moving' sand dunes became a problem with white settlement. Cook wrote of them being at the water's edge, flanked by tall trees and shrubbery. Birnie started the degradation and by 1860 there were no trees left to hold the sand between Kurnell and North Cronulla. With no windbreak, onshore gales started the dunes moving inland. Sydney sand companies completed the job by mining what was left for the Sydney building trade.*

(8) On the left is the memorial to Forby Sutherland, a seaman on the *Endeavour*, who was the first recorded British subject to be buried on Australian soil. Much discussion followed over the exact spot of his grave, but it appears his skull was found near Cook's creek. If you look closely in front of Sutherland's monument, you can see where Birnie cut a shipping dock through the flat rock. His only means of moving produce was by sea. The channel is easy to see at low tide, and is a popular paddling pool.

(9) The granite obelisk remembers Dr Daniel Carl Solander, a Swedish naturalist and personal friend of Banks who faithfully recorded Australia's strange fauna and flora with sketches and descriptions. Unfortunately Solander died suddenly before his work was finished and it was never published as intended. To

this day it remains in the vault of the British Museum.

(10) Further east is a red buoy showing where the *Endeavour* anchored and there's a plaque on the rocks honouring the scientific endeavour of the expedition. The area is now a popular scuba-diving and snorkelling spot.
Go back to Solander's monument and head towards the sealed road leading to the right of the brick building with steps in the front. This is the

Discovery Centre, open from 11 am to 3 pm Monday to Friday, and 10 am to 4.30 pm at weekends. There are two permanent exhibitions here that are well worth a look. 'Eight Days that Changed the World' tells of Cook's impact and exploration of Botany Bay and his relationship with the Aborigines, and 'Wetlands Reflections' focuses on nearby Towra Point's wetlands and its importance to migrating wader birds.

(11) **On the other side of the Discovery Centre car park the Yena Track heads south-east.** Notice the twisted limbs of the beautiful salmon-coloured *Angophora costata* — the Sydney red gum. The Aborigines used to make coolamons from the dead 'elbows' to carry water or food.

About 150 metres after the Solander-Banks loop, five tracks converge. The right-hand one goes about 50 metres up the hill for a spectacular view of the oil refinery. The Caltex Oil Refinery started production here in the mid-1950s but not without a fight. Sutherland Shire Council was against the development chiefly because Cook's landing place was hallowed ground, plus the only access was by horse-drawn carriage or ferry from La Perouse, and Kurnell wasn't on mains water. The refinery was

> *The actual siting of the Caltex Oil Refinery was finally made on the deck of the local ferry. It appears nature took its revenge for the official neglect of Kurnell and the lack of a road during anniversary celebrations in 1949. Some 500 dignitaries had been deposited by launch on the beach when a mini-cyclone sprang up, shredding the bunting and soaking the guests. It was so rough the governor couldn't land and the visitors were marooned. Even the air force evacuation trucks bogged in the sand, and the guard of honour had to march out through the dunes into the teeth of the gale.*

> *Weeds have always been a problem in the national park, but by far the most aggressive is the South African bitou bush, with its insatiable appetite for space. The invasive lantana of 20 years ago is described as a pussycat compared with this succulent, light green plant. Its tiny green berries are scattered by birds and foxes and the seeds survive in the soil for about seven years. It's also a tree killer, out-competing others twice its size. Incidentally, the bitou was introduced into Australia to stabilise sandhills!*

finally given the go ahead, which was sanctioned by an act of parliament, but on the condition it paid for and built a road from Cronulla. Captain Cook Drive, costing 180,000 pounds, was through by June 1953, and by February 1956 Caltex was pumping oil across Botany Bay to its Banksmeadow storage and distribution depot.

Retrace your steps and continue on the Yena Track. When you reach the sealed road turn right and stay on it until you reach the Cape Solander car park.

(12) **Leave the car park and walk south along the cliff tops.** Take your children firmly by the hand and don't go too close to the edge. (If you look down the coast you can see where whole rock shelfs have fallen off!) The track winds over sandstone ledges and beside low-growing banksia, baeckea and *casuarina*

(she-oaks). New Holland and white-cheeked honeyeaters, red wattlebirds and crimson rosellas feed on the heathland flowers, while golden-headed cisticolas, cuckoos and shy emu-wrens can also be seen darting around the shrubbery. About 200 million years ago the Sydney sandstone was formed when this coastline was part of a huge delta. Thick layers of sand deposits hardened in time, forming the present cliffs. The rocks still have a sandy touch.

(13) **The track veers inland at a gorge after about 20 minutes from the car park; you will come to a pipeline-like fence. Tabbagai Gap** is one of several gorges along the coastline formed about 50 million years ago after volcanic activity. Long ridges of basalt rock weathered faster than the sandstone, leaving deep ravines. If you look closely you can see the remains of the fishermen's shacks on the south-eastern side of the gap. Half a dozen or so were built into the cliff and connected by steps. Some were quite elaborate, with cupboards and beds etched out of the rock. Some had elementary plumbing and one fisherman lived here permanently. Around 1970 the Tabbagai cliff dwellers were moved out and their shacks dismantled. Oil refinery effluent is piped into the sea here, and it was a dumping ground for stolen cars, thus spoiling its natural beauty.

Cross over Tabbagai Gap and follow the arrows back to the cliff top. The vegetation here is shorter still because of the harsh salty conditions. Grey-coloured coastal rosemary, wild fuchsia and honey myrtles dot the landscape. These plants have small, waxy, shiny leaves to help prevent water loss, and deep roots to search for water. They also do well after a bushfire.

Birds to look for along the cliff tops are the common and crested terns, with their black heads; muttonbirds; young Australasian gannets, fresh from breeding grounds in New Zealand, which could be shoalfishing offshore; white-breasted eagles; albatrosses, which come close to shore after a southeasterly storm; the rare peregrine falcon, which swoops on its prey at 300 kilometres an hour; the not-so-speedy kestrel, which might be gliding above waiting to pounce on a

The Cronulla sandhills provided the setting for the movie 40,000 Horsemen, the story of the greatest cavalry charge in modern times. About 500 horses raced through the dunes, re-enacting the charge of the Australian Light Horse at Beersheba in the First World War. The charge was led by Lieutenant General Sir Henry Chauvel, uncle of Charles Chauvel, the producer and director. The movie was popular in England and the United States as well as Australia, and helped develop the 'Aussie digger' image.

small heathland animal; and the little rock warbler, which suspends its nest from rock caverns.

(14) Blue Hole Gorge is the next impediment on the track. Before you head off around it, peer over — with caution! It's 30 metres deep. Walk up the side of the gorge and keep turning left, but stay high enough to skirt the swamp at the top. The bush might be a bit thick, but push through. If you have trouble finding the right path, remember the aim is to get back to the cliff top on the other side. The National Parks and Wildlife Service is signing and upgrading these tracks and blocking off old ones. Hopefully the work will be finished in time for your walk, making directions clearer.

Blue Hole Gorge is the largest of several freshwater swamps on the walk, providing a watering ground for snakes, birds and other animals, and an important breeding ground for frogs and insects. The 'tinkling' frog, so named because of the noise it makes, is a small, brown endangered species found here.

There is yet one more ravine to round. Follow the totem markers back to the cliff top and head for the lighthouse.

(15) Follow the track to the Cape Baily Lighthouse, and climb up. To the northwest is Solander Trig, the highest point on the peninsula, 67 metres above sea level. There were some minor military fortifications up here during the Second World War, but they've since been buried.

Resting 800 metres out to sea off the lighthouse lie the remains of the steamer Hilda, 25 metres down on a reef. The Hilda was on her regular run from Coalcliff near Wollongong to Sydney on a perfectly clear night in 1893, when she ran aground off Cape Baily. There was a dispute between the helmsman and the captain over the Hilda's course. As a result of the accident, the captain lost his master's licence for three months and the helmsman won an honourable seaman's discharge. The embarrassed crew rowed 8 kilometres to Botany Bay and walked back to Sydney.

The Trig Track has been closed because of a 'blow out'. This occurs when the vegetative cover disappears, the track deepens, the sides fall in and the sand blows out and leaves a huge hole sometimes 15 metres deep. The marching sand dune smothers everything in its path as it drifts across the countryside, creating a real problem which can cost more than $100,000 to fix.

(16) **Potter Point can be identified by the four large pipes pointing skywards.** These are breather stacks from the Cronulla Sewerage Works, venting some of the gases before the screened effluent is pumped into the sea.

Boat Harbour, just around the corner, has suffered from the pollution, but the sewerage works are being upgraded. This area has been seriously eroded by trailbike riders.

Continue on to Potter Point if you want, staying near the cliff edge, or retrace your steps to the Discovery Centre and catch the bus back to Cronulla station.

WALK 25

PARRAMATTA

START POINT:	Parramatta ferry, Phillip Street.
FINISH:	Parramatta ferry, Phillip Street.
HOW TO GET THERE:	By rivercat from Circular Quay.
LENGTH:	5.5 kilometres.
WALKING TIME:	1.75 hours.
ACTUAL TIME:	Allow all day.
RATING:	An easy, mostly flat walk along sealed footpaths and roads.
WEATHER CHECK:	Suitable wet or fine.
REFRESHMENTS:	There are abundant cafes, food and drink shops and restaurants.

Suitable for wheelchairs and strollers.

*P*arramatta, the thriving centre of western Sydney, is steeped in history. It boasts over 90 historic buildings and sites and many 'firsts'. This pretty walk threads its way from one end of town to the other, past beautifully restored buildings, through leafy green parkland and beside its first 'lifeblood', the gently flowing river. In February 1788 Governor Arthur Phillip set sail from Port Jackson in search of the source of the river, but more importantly, to find arable land to grow crops for his fledgling colony in Sydney. Two months later he discovered Parramatta, which he initially named the Crescent because of the shape of the hill behind the present Old Government House. The new town he named Rose Hill after Sir George Rose, Secretary to the Treasury in England. Convicts cleared the land and on 2 November 1788 the foundations of the second white settlement in Australia were laid at Parramatta Park. Rose Hill was later given its Aboriginal name *Parramatta*, meaning 'The place where eels lie down' or 'head of the river' — a dispute remains about which it is. It was also called the 'cradle city' because of its number of firsts. Parramatta grew rapidly and within ten years promised to become the new centre of the colony. It has the oldest government building, old Government House; the oldest private home, John and Elizabeth Macarthur's Elizabeth Farm; the first experimental farm; the first successful harvest; the first land grant, gaol, vineyard, woollen mill, legal brewery, horseracing meeting etc. In 1938 Parramatta was given city status and is now the commercial centre of the great suburban sprawl westwards.

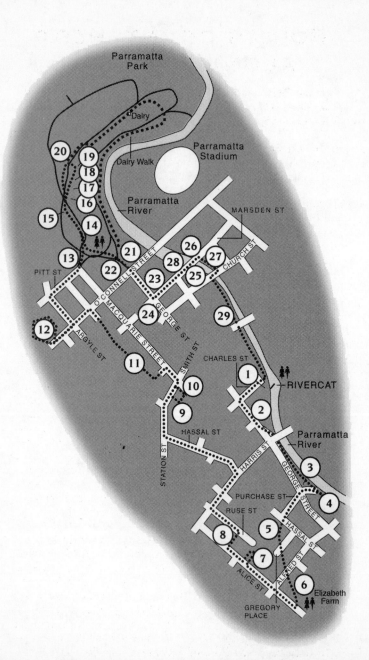

Parramatta Park

Dairy

Dairy Walk

Parramatta Stadium

Parramatta River

MARSDEN ST

PITT ST

O'CONNELL STREET

MACQUARIE STREET

ARGYLE ST

GEORGE ST

CHURCH ST

SMITH ST

CHARLES ST

RIVERCAT

STATION ST

HASSAL ST

Parramatta River

HARRIS ST

GEORGE STREET

PURCHASE ST

RUSE ST

HASSAL ST

ALFRED ST

ALICE ST

GREGORY PLACE

Elizabeth Farm

POINTS OF INTEREST ALONG THE WAY

(1) **From the ferry, head off down Charles Street then turn left into George Street.**

(2) **Harrisford, at 182 George Street,** is the original site of the Kings School which opened in 1832 to educate the sons of wealthy farmers, merchants and government officials. The Kings boys moved to their new school on the north side of the river four years later, but this building continued to be used for schooling until bought by a descendant of Surgeon John Harris who changed the name to Harrisford. The Kings Old Boys' Association restored Harrisford for the school's 150th anniversary, and today it's a commercial premises.

The first contact between the Aborigines and whites was cautious. The Aborigines were perplexed by the European's skin colour, clothes, transport and guns. The first settlers couldn't understand the natives' philosophy — they had no regard for material things, they didn't build houses or churches and had no farms. They thought the Aborigines were ignorant and dangerous, even though they were extremely tolerant of the whites. There were hostilities, usually started by the British and followed with retaliatory action by the Aborigines.

(3) **On the edge of the river stood the Queens Wharf, originally known as The Landing Place,** built by convicts from gum trees and rebuilt with sandstone by David Lennox in 1835 — four years before he built his namesake further upstream.

(4) **Two memorials** to the men and officers who served on the three naval vessels bearing the name *Parramatta* stand beside the river. *Parramatta* II was sunk by a German U-boat during the Second World War with the loss of 138 lives.

(5) **Hambledon Cottage** was built by John Macarthur in 1824 on his Elizabeth Farm property for his daughters' governess Penelope Lucas. The colonial Georgian-style cottage, built of rendered sandstock brick, was joined in Australian cedar, and one bedroom still has its ironbark floors. Macarthur's oldest son Edward Macarthur was its first occupant, followed by family friend Archdeacon Thomas Hobbes Scott. Penelope Lucas, called Aunt or Mrs Lucas out of courtesy by the children, moved to Hambledon in her retirement. She named the cottage after the town in England and lived here until her death in 1836. The building was eventually bought by the Whitehall Pharmaceutical Company and donated to the

Parramatta City Council, which restored it. The local historical society now opens Hamledon Cottage from Wednesday to Sunday and on most public holidays at 11 am to 4 pm for a modest fee.

(6) Continue down Gregory Place, turn left down the path by the canal and cross the road. Go right over the canal bridge and walk diagonally across the park to Elizabeth Farm in Alice Street. Elizabeth Farm house was built in 1793 by John Macarthur, named after his wife and is the oldest standing house in Australia. It is a charming example of the first Australian colonial-style farmhouse, built on a 40 hectare grant of the best land in Parramatta. With the help of convict labour Macarthur developed and diversified. His

John Macarthur was a bad-tempered, eccentric, innovative man, who became extremely wealthy from his business ventures. He made enemies of everyone, and when he wasn't arguing with governors or fighting duels, he was back in England in political exile. However, his vision that Australia would rise to greatness on the sheep's back, merinos in particular, was correct. John was declared a lunatic and died under house arrest. Through all this, Elizabeth managed the properties, raised the children, charmed the governors and nurtured a magnificent garden at Elizabeth Farm.

grant soon became 202 hectares, then thousands of hectares with the addition of Cowpastures and Toongabbie — an estate that rivalled the governor's. Elizabeth Farm is open every day from 10 am to 5 pm; $5 adults, $3 pensioners, $12 families.

(7) Walk down Alice Street, cross Alfred Street and on top of the hill is Our Lady of Lebanon Church. You must have noticed the statue of Our Lady, surrounded by symbolic praying hands, on the skyline. This exquisite circular church was built by the local Lebanese community. It seats 1300, has an Australian cedar dome, central altar and beautifully handcrafted stained glass windows depicting the patron saints from different villages in Lebanon. About 40,000 Maronite Catholics from throughout the Western Suburbs congregate here. The door is usually open

(8) Continue down Alice Street and turn right through a little park to Experimental Farm, where ex-convict farmer James Ruse was given a grant of 0.6 hectares to see if he could make it self-sufficient. It was imperative the experiment work as Governor Phillip was yet to find fertile land to feed the more than 1000 mouths of the First Fleet. Ruse's only help was his wife Elizabeth Perry, who was the first woman convict in New South Wales to be emancipated. Ruse was successful and sold his holding to

Experimental Farm cottage has a resident ghost. Not one in a white shroud, but one that makes its presence felt. An architrave flew off a bookshelf in the second bedroom, landing 4 metres across the room: the lights go up and down, and the hackles of an attendant's dog stand on end when it's near the cellar. A man is believed to have died there.

Surgeon John Harris, who built the cottage on this site. Harris became a wealthy settler, owning land in the suburb now known as Harris Park, and his main estate was at Ultimo.

⑨ Follow the map and just past the junction of Station and Smith streets you will come to the Lancer Barracks, Australia's oldest continuously used military establishment.

Originally built in Governor Macquarie's time in 1818, the barracks resounded to the movements of the British redcoats until the colonial force was formed in the 1860s. Two of the three original buildings remain: the two-storey sandstone brick accommodation block for 100 soldiers and the single-storey officers' quarters. In 1891 Lancer Barracks became the home of the Parramatta Half Squadron of the famous New South Wales Lancers. Horses have given way to wheels, and today it's the headquarters of the Armoured Reconnaissance Regiment of the Army Reserve. Lovely little Linden House on the other side of the parade ground was faithfully rebuilt stone by stone from its Macquarie Street site and is now a military museum. Linden House was originally Governor Darling's School of Industry, where girls

were taught domestic arts and given basic schooling. Linden House opens on Sundays only, from 11 am to 4 pm.

⑩ Just around the corner in Macquarie Street is the Arthur Phillip old schoolhouse. Built in 1875 in Victorian Gothic style, complete with belltower and spire, this school was the oldest public school in the Parramatta district. Now a museum, it's open only one day a month.

⑪ Continue down Macquarie Street and left into Civic Place. Go down beside the council chambers and the quaint pink town hall to the Church Street Mall and St John's Cathedral. The first church services in Parramatta were held in the open air, and the first churches were two wooden huts built in 1796 on the corner of George and Marsden streets. Reverend Samuel Marsden was the minister. He moved on to St John's when the foundation stone was laid in 1802, but also rode into town each week to preach at St Philip's at The Rocks. St John's wasn't finished until 1820 when the two spires were added, but fell into disrepair and was replaced with the present cathedral in 1855. The fiery Samuel Marsden preached hell and damnation from the three-tiered pulpit until his death in 1838. The mall was a marketplace in the 1800s and in 1816 Governor Macquarie held a feast for the local Aborigines, which became an annual event so popular that 300 turned up in 1819.

12 Next stop is St John's cemetery in O'Connell Street, behind the convict-built wall, almost 1 kilometre from St John's. Originally it was a public burial ground, but later became Anglican. Henry Edward Dodd, superintendent of convicts at Parramatta, lies here. His grave, dated 1791, is the oldest marked grave in Australia. Only 14 people had died before the arrival of the Second Fleet, and with their arrival came disease and a dramatic increase in the number of deaths. Wander around the graves — there are many famous First Fleeters here, Samuel Marsden and John Harris among them. There are the graves of John Blaxland, who arrived with his brother in their own boat in 1806 with all the necessary equipment to start Australia's cattle industry; Baron Augustus Theodore Henry Alt, the first Surveyor-General; John Batman,

---

The new settlers were having trouble not only with the Aborigines, but their own population as well. In 1804 under the slogan 'liberty or death', the Irish 'croppies' decided to storm Parramatta, seize some ships and escape. Word of the revolt preceded them and they marched into the clutches of the New South Wales Corps. Fifteen were shot dead, nine were court-martialled and hanged and the rest were flogged and sent to the Newcastle coalmines, ending one of the more violent episodes in Australian history.

---

the founder of Melbourne; and William Cosgrove, who was killed by bushrangers.

Go back down O'Connell Street, left into Argyle and right into Pitt Street and where it doglegs right, enter Parramatta Park.

13 Immediately on your left is the Gatehouse Art Gallery. There were gatehouses at the five entrances to the park with a park ranger living in each. This particular one was restored by Parramatta City Council as a bicentenary project and is now leased by the local art society. The gallery is open on Sundays from 10 am to 4 pm; admission is free.

14 Walk up the centre road to Old Government House, originally built of lathe and plaster for Governor Phillip in 1790. It soon fell into disrepair and was replaced by Governor Hunter with an elegant Georgian house in 1799. Governor Macquarie built a two-storey block at the back and two one-storey wings on each side. A timber portico, probably designed by Francis Greenway, was added and the house as it stands today was completed in 1818. Massive vegetable gardens were planted in front of the house, and in surrounding paddocks wheat, maize and barley were grown, plus a vineyard and citrus orchard. The various governors enjoyed staying at Parramatta, but when the new Government House opened in

Sydney in 1845, this one again fell into disrepair through lack of funds. In 1857 the land was proclaimed a public park, the house rented by various schools, and eventually restored by the National Trust. It's open every day except Monday from 10 am to 4 pm.

⑮ At the top of the hill on the left is the site of Governor Brisbane's Observatory.

Governor Brisbane, an expert astronomer, made Parramatta his chief residence, and in 1822 built an observatory at his own expense. His two astronomers, Luis Rumker and James Dunlop, set about recording every visible star in the southern hemisphere — 7385 were charted and a staggering 40,000 sighted.

⑯ Over the road Governor Brisbane built a bathhouse,

no doubt here because he spent so much time at his observatory. The bathhouse was enclosed, had several cubicles, evidence remains of a fireplace and the water was pumped from the river below. Governor Brisbane suffered from arthritis and he used this bathhouse to ease his pain.

⑰ Under constant threat of attack from the Aborigines, Governor Phillip built a redoubt or fort to protect the early settlers.

One infamous Aboriginal, Burnham Pemulwuy, led a 12-year campaign of terror in true guerilla style. His own people believed he was immortal, and the early settlers lived in fear. In 1797 Pemulwuy took on more than 100 redcoats at Toongabbie and those that weren't killed retreated to Parramatta for the next onslaught. Pemulwuy was shot seven times, and with massive head wounds was taken to Parramatta Hospital, where he was expected to die. Not only did he survive, but he escaped in chains. After several more incursions, Pemulwuy was killed in a police ambush in 1902. His head was pickled and sent to London with word the natives had been subdued.

(18) Towering over everything is the Boer War memorial which incorporates columns and stones from the first Parramatta Courthouse, designed by colonial architect Mortimer Lewis in Greek Revival style.

(19) Running in front of the memorial is all that's left of the old steam tram, which was similar to the one that ran down George Street. The old tram mysteriously caught fire. The huge lightstands you can see above the treetops to the north mark the home of the Parramatta Eels, the local rugby league club. It was on this site that the Cumberland Turf Club built its racecourse in 1847. Incidentally, the first race meeting was held in Parramatta in 1810.

(20) On the western side of the road is a memorial to William Ewart Hart, a Parramatta dentist who made the first cross-country flight in Australia flying from Penrith to Parramatta in just 19 minutes. He landed his aircraft here in 1911. The next year he started his own aviation company on a site he considered to be 'the finest from an aviation viewpoint in Australia'. Today that site is the RAAF base at Richmond!

If you feel like adding a 2 kilometre loop and 25 minutes to your walk keep going, but with the knowledge you have another 2 kilometres to get back to the ferry. Follow the tramline until you get to two white cottages. The older of the two was the governor's dairy, run by emancipist Elizabeth Eccles, who died at the formidable age of 105. She made cheeses, skimmed the cream, churned the butter and dispensed milk to the nearby households. **Follow the cottage fence to the road below, turn right and walk beside the river to the George Street gates.**

(21) For those who aren't visiting the dairy, retrace your steps down the hill. On the left just before the George Street gatehouse is an obelisk under a tree to Lady Mary Fitzroy, wife of Governor Fitzroy, who was thrown to her death from her carriage in 1847 when the horses bolted. Following the tragedy, Fitzroy returned to Sydney. He was the last governor to use the vice-regal residence.

(22) **Walk out through the Tower Gates built** in 1885 — Governor Phillip's original entrance to the park — **and cross O'Connell Street into George Street,** the main street in town, initially linking the river and Government House.

(23) **On the northwestern corner of George Street and Marsden Street is Brislington,** the oldest existing domestic dwelling in Parramatta, built by emancipated convict John Hodges in 1821. Legend has it Hodges won 1000 pounds in a euchre game with the eight of diamonds and incorporated the diamond shape in the back wall of the house. He was later caught paying convicts with rum, sentenced to hard labour and had his house confiscated. The house was bought by Dr Walter Brown in 1857 who named it Brislington after a suburb in Bristol. Here began a dynasty of Doctors Brown who gave more than 90 years' continuous medical service to Parramatta. It is now a museum open the first and third Sunday of each month, and the second and last Thursday from 10.30 am to 3.30 pm.

(24) **Diagonally opposite is the Woolpack Hotel,** which holds the longest continuous licence in Australia and began where the courts are today as Woolpack Inn, the city's most famous hotel. It was first called the Freemason's Arms in 1798 and renamed the Woolpack Inn when James Nash became publican in 1821. Wealthy farmers stayed there; it was fashionable with honeymooners and it became a famous holiday spot. The rich freeborn settlers or 'true merinos' wanted to preserve the class barrier at all costs and boycotted Governor Brisbane's farewell dinner because they wouldn't want to sit with ex-convicts.

(25) **Turn left into Marsden Street and when you cross the Parramatta River look right at the Lennox Street bridge,** a beautiful stone structure built in 1839 by stonemason David Lennox for almost 1800 pounds. It remained unchanged for almost a century when it was unsympathetically altered to carry more vehicular traffic and trams.

For breakfast and tea the Kings boys ate dry bread, washed down by basins of green tea sweetened by brown sugar to the colour of coffee. Dinner was always beef — boiled one day and roasted the next, and sometimes accompanied by duff, a suet pudding made with inch-thick lard. Discipline was brutal with floggings dished out by senior boys, and naughty boys were suspended from the ceiling in a cage. Heavy drinking was the norm and publicans were known to keep prostitutes on the premises so older boys could have 'a bit on the side'.

(26) **On your left is Laurel House,** the Kings School's masters' accommodation, which grew from a cottage to a large house like the laurel trees beside it, which gave it its name. The Kings School opened here in 1836 with accommodation for 60 boarders and 40 day boys. The days began at 7.00 in the morning and continued to 9.00 at night, the boys' time devoted to classical studies and religion. Despite many additions Kings eventually outgrew the premises and moved to a new site in northeastern Parramatta.

(27) **On the river is the Riverside Theatres,** the cultural centre of Parramatta, built as a bicentenary project in 1988.

(28) **Walk across Prince Alfred Park and turn right into Church Street. On the Lennox Street Bridge look upstream to the Parramatta Weir,** which stops the fresh water mixing with the tidal salty water. The weir was built in 1818 to provide a fresh water supply for the town, and householders could have their casks replenished from the dam for 6 pence to 1 shilling.

(29) **Cross the road and take the steps on the southeastern corner of the bridge down to the river path. Follow it back to the ferry.**